T0326808

COURTS AND TRIALS:
A MULTIDISCIPLINARY APPROACH

M.L. FRIEDLAND is dean of the Faculty of Law, University of Toronto, and the author of *Detention Before Trial, Cases and Materials on Criminal Law and Procedure, Double Jeopardy*, and a number of periodical articles and government reports.

The judicial system occupies an important place in society, yet it has been one of the least-studied of Canadian institutions. Traditionally, examination and criticism of the trial process have been left to lawyers and members of the legal profession. In this volume nine non-lawyers scrutinize its operation in Canada from the perspectives of several academic disciplines.

Reginald Allen, a philosopher and classicist, discusses the modern trial process in the light of the trial of Socrates; Anatol Rapoport, a mathematician noted for his work in the fields of game theory and conflict resolution, analyses the adversary system from a Marxist perspective; Anthony Doob, a psychologist, examines the rules of evidence;

Charles Hanly, a philosopher and psychoanalyst, uses the *Truscott* case to explore the psychopathological aspects of a trial from a Freudian viewpoint; one political scientist, Peter Russell, examines the courts' role in the development of the law; another, Donald Smiley, studies their role as protectors of civil liberties; James Giffen, a sociologist, points out the inadequacy of the criminal justice system as a means of controlling alcohol and drug addiction; Donald Dewees, an economist, examines court regulation of economic behaviour; and Kenneth McNaught, a historian, discusses the political trial in the Canadian legal system.

The papers were originally presented as a series of lectures sponsored by the Faculty of Law at the University of Toronto. This book is a first step in the vital task of removing the legal process from isolation as the special province of lawyers and making it more responsive to contemporary problems and concerns.

EDITED BY MARTIN L. FRIEDLAND

Courts and Trials:
a multidisciplinary approach

UNIVERSITY OF TORONTO PRESS
TORONTO AND BUFFALO

© University of Toronto Press 1975
Toronto and Buffalo
Reprinted in paperback 2017
ISBN 978-0-8020-2188-5 (cloth)
ISBN 978-0-8020-6273-4 (paper)

LIBRARY OF CONGRESS CATALOGING IN PUBLICATION DATA
Main entry under title:
Courts and trials.
Includes bibliographical references.
1. Judicial process — Canada — Addresses, essays, lectures.
2. Courts — Canada — Addresses, essays, lectures.   1 Friedland, Martin L.
Law   347'.73   75-5672
ISBN 978-0-8020-2188-5 (bound)   ISBN 978-0-8020-6273-4 (pbk.)

This book has been published with the
help of a grant from the Social Science
Research Council of Canada, using funds
provided by the Canada Council.

To Bora Laskin

Contents

Preface

The judicial system occupies an important place in society. Yet it has been one of the least studied of all Canadian institutions.

Non-lawyers in Canada have for the most part left the task to lawyers. Lawyers, with a few notable exceptions, have not produced anything of significance. One can only speculate as to why non-lawyers have not studied the legal process. Perhaps it was felt to be too difficult for non-lawyers to pierce the veil of mystery surrounding the law; perhaps it was the difficulty of getting information about the legal system; or perhaps it was the risk of a citation for contempt if the writer went too far in criticizing the courts.

The purpose of this collection of papers, which arose out of a series of talks given in the Faculty of Law in 1972–3 by non-lawyers at the University of Toronto, is – to put it quite simply – to show that non-lawyers can make a significant contribution to the study of legal institutions. Each paper looks at the judicial system from a different perspective and thereby gives the reader a better understanding of the institution studied.

The first paper – by a philosopher and classicist, Reginald Allen – shows through an analysis of the trial of Socrates that many of the problems that confront us today concerning the trial process have confronted society for many, many years. Professor Allen reminds us that 'change is not, at least by definition, change for the good' and urges us to make sure that 'the values of legality and procedural fairness ... be kept clearly and steadily before the mind in any discussion of law reform.'

Another historical approach to the subject – this time from a Marxist perspective – is taken in the next paper, 'Theories of conflict resolution and the law,' by Anatol Rapoport, a mathematician noted for his work in the fields of game theory and conflict resolution, who takes the position that the court system mirrors the dominant values in society. According to Professor Rapoport, the adversary system, like the capitalist system, is based on a laissez faire approach in which justice is assumed to emerge through the clash of competing interests.

The growth of the social sciences and other disciplines has now provided us with some tools with which to test and analyse the functioning of our court procedures. For example, Anthony Doob shows in his paper, 'Psychology and evidence,' that a psychologist has much to contribute to a discussion on reform of the law of evidence. His studies indicate that some of our rules of evidence cannot stand up to critical scientific examination. Similarly, Charles Hanly, a philosopher and psychoanalyst, in his paper, 'Psychopathology of the trial process,' analyses the well-known *Truscott* case and argues that Freudian analysis can be applied to the trial process. 'It is reasonable to assume' states Professor Hanly 'that the venerability and sanctity of the law do not immunize jurors, lawyers, and judges against the influence of unconscious processes while in court.' Both Professors Doob and Hanly make the important point that a recent amendment to the Criminal Code, which prohibits jurors from discussing what went on in the jury room, makes it virtually impossible to do effective scientific research into the jury system. Surely it would be reasonable to provide an exception in the legislation for scientific enquiry.

The courts have an important role to play in the development of the law. Peter Russell, a political scientist, shows this in his paper, 'Judicial power in Canada's political culture.' He urges us to recognize that courts exercise political power and that we should find ways of making it legitimate rather than denying its existence. Donald Smiley, another political scientist, is concerned about extending judicial power into the controversial area of the protection of human rights. It would be a mistake, argues Professor Smiley in his paper, 'Courts, legislatures, and the protection of human rights,' to leave the protection of human rights to the courts and in particular to entrench the Canadian Bill of Rights in the Constitution.

We then turn to some specific uses of the law. James Giffen, a sociologist, in his paper, 'The criminal courts and the control of addictions,' looks at the use of the court system to control alcoholism and drug addiction. In this area the courts have not been particularly effective, but as Professor Giffen points out, 'once law enforcement has been established through usage as the method of dealing with what comes to be defined as a serious danger, public resistance to change tends to create an institutional inertia.' This is certainly the case with narcotics addiction, although in the case of alcoholism steps are being taken to explore other alternatives to the 'revolving-door' treatment.

Similarly, the courts have not been effective in regulating the economy. As a result, for many matters the state has turned to administrative agencies. However, Donald Dewees, an economist with legal training, feels that the courts could play an important role in economic regulation if they would adopt a more sophisticated analysis of penalties to ensure that 'crime does not pay.' As Professor Dewees points out in his paper, 'The courts and economic regulation,' 'reasonable controls combined with penalties proportional to the harm done can ... be quite effective.'

In one area, however, the court system, according to historian Kenneth McNaught, has been effective, and that is political trials. Professor McNaught traces the history of these trials in his paper, 'Political trials and the Canadian political tradition,' and states that 'when one considers the aftermath of political crises and trials in Canada, from Mackenzie and Papineau, to some of the spies unmasked by Igor Gouzenko, and on to Pierre Vallières, one might conclude that few countries have witnessed the repentance of such a high proportion of political rebels.' Professor McNaught goes on to speculate whether 'a major reason for this has been the combination of firm action and succeeding lenience which seems to characterize our basically conservative political-judicial tradition.'

The series of papers is not meant to be comprehensive. There are obvious gaps: to take just a single example, one would have liked to have had an anthropologist look at our court system. The subtitle originally proposed for this book was 'an interdisciplinary perspective,' but this was changed to 'a multidisciplinary approach' in recognition of the fact that this book is a collection of separate perspectives from a variety of points of view, and no attempt has been made by the authors or by the editor in this preface to relate the various papers to each other. We are still a long way from an effective integration of the experience of different disciplines in the study of legal problems.

I hope that this series will serve to stimulate other non-lawyers – and lawyers – to study the legal system.

M L F

COURTS AND TRIALS:
A MULTIDISCIPLINARY APPROACH

REGINALD ALLEN

The trial of Socrates: a study in the morality of the criminal process

A Platonist asked to contribute to a series of seminars on law reform, and specifically courts and trials, finds himself in an honoured but onerous position. To speak intelligently of reform requires, in the first place, thorough knowledge of the present state of the law, a theme best left to lawyers. It requires, in the second place, well-grounded opinion about the present effects of law on the lives of those toward whom it is directed and the probable consequences of change – a subject to which economics, sociology, and statistics are surely relevant and practical experience in the administration of law vital. Neither training nor experience qualify me to speak with authority on either point.

Yet the very notion of law reform assumes that the present state of the law may be made better and therefore, presumably, that it may also be made worse. We are far enough along in the twentieth century to question with some asperity the myth of perpetual progress, and if we need not therefore return to the ancient myth of cyclical regress, we may at least suppose that change is not, at least by definition, change for the good.

Certainly in respect to the criminal process, the voices raised on behalf of change these days are numerous and insistent. Leaving aside the continuing debate about what the process is for – whether punishment, as distinct from reformation, is a legitimate aim or instrument of law, or again, whether the substantive content of the criminal law sets appropriate limits to what shall and shall not be made criminal – there is considerable criticism of the process itself. Whether we look to the rules of evidence, to procedure, or to the very institution of jury trial, the story is the same: the trial process is condemned as clumsy and inefficient, an arcane plaything for lawyers, an only slightly civilized substitute for trial by combat, in which the weapons used are words. The cluster of legal values compendiously summed up under the heading of 'the adversary system' is increasingly under attack. A trial, it is said, ought to be a search for truth; instead, it is often a game. A judge ought wisely to dispense justice; instead, he is often a referee.

That there is truth in all this is too plain to be denied; things human carry with them imperfection. But it is worth remembering that half of a whole truth is often equivalent to a very great falsehood and that the law is often complex because it deals with issues of very great complexity, attempting to reconcile, in a wise balance, diverse and conflicting interests and ideals. Thus, for example, if one major aim of trial is truth, another aim is protection of individual liberty. Both aims are neatly consistent – in the abstract. But this hardly settles the question, let us say, of what use shall be made in a court of law of a confession extracted by torture. It is not by accident that the history of constitutional law, from chapter twenty-nine of Magna Carta to the Petition of Right, the Habeas Corpus Act, and the bills of rights – English, American, Canadian – may very largely be written as a history of criminal procedure. It is in the criminal process that law and government most narrowly touch, beneficently and also dangerously, the lives of the governed. And it is here that instinct and passion beat hardest on rationality and restraint.

Much of the apparent inefficiency of the criminal process derives from limitations on the reach of law. Indeed, it is plausible to suppose that those limitations are instruments for providing, prospectively and under circumstances of foreseen stress, concrete embodiment of ideals implicit in the very nature of law itself. There is the ideal of procedural fairness: that no free man – *nullus liber homo* – shall be subject to penal liability without notice and an opportunity to be heard before an impartial tribunal. There is a substantive ideal, often called the principle of legality: that no free man shall be subject to penal liability imposed retroactively or except according to a clearly defined standard of wrong. It is arguable that these ideals are implied in the very enterprise of law, and that limitations provide them with practical and institutionalized expression. Limitation, of course, is always in some sense inefficient; yet this sort of limitation enters into the very definition of what, at law, is to be understood by truth with respect to a verdict.

The principle of legality and the ideal of procedural fairness are directly and intimately connected. However it may be in metaphysics, adjectives in law determine the effects of substance, as substance does of adjectives. The main vice excluded by the principle of legality is often taken to be retroactivity; in fact, I suggest, it is vagueness, for vagueness bears on proof. Notice of a vague charge, though it may allow you to prepare a defence that rests on persuasion – rhetoric – will not allow a defence that rests on proof, for there can be no proof where there is no clear standard of wrongdoing. A tribunal asked to adjudicate a vague charge can scarcely be called impartial: impartiality is not exhibited by disinterested coin-flipping. On the other hand, the principle of legality loses its sense apart from notice and hearing before an impartial tribunal. In short, where the principle of legality is not honoured, procedural fairness is lost, even when it is, on the surface, provided for. As a concrete example of this, I offer a very famous, and ancient, trial.

In the year 399 BC, in Athens, Socrates son of Sophroniscus, of the deme Alopece, aged seventy, was brought to trial on a writ of impiety, a *graphe asebeias*. He was found guilty and condemned to death.

It was, of course, a celebrated case, and for years afterward controversy swirled around the verdict. The author of the *Seventh Epistle*, who may or may not have been Plato, writing some forty years after the fact; described Socrates as the best and most righteous man of his time and dismissed the charge of impiety as one which he, *least* of all men, deserved. Whether or not those are Plato's own words, they most certainly represent Plato's own views and those of many other Athenians. Yet Socrates died a condemned criminal.

The history books tell us that 'in equity Socrates was innocent. In Attic law he was guilty of the charge preferred against him.'[1] Let us see.

Certainly Socrates was guilty if guilt is construed formally to follow on being found guilty. No irregularity in the proceedings was remarked either at the time or afterward. And in appearance, at least, the fundamental requirements of procedural fairness were met. There was notice, hearing, and, to the degree that Athenian law could provide it, an impartial tribunal.

Notice was provided formally, by personal service and sworn indictment. The indictment has been preserved for us by Diogenes Laertius on the authority of the Hellenistic scholar Favorinus, who searched the Athenian archives and found it there: 'This indictment is sworn by Meletus, son of Meletus of Pitthos, against Socrates, son of Sophroniscus of Alopece: Socrates is guilty of not acknowledging the gods acknowledged by the City,

---

1 Hammond, *A History of Greece* (2d ed, 1967), at 449, following, with greater caution, Bury, *History of Greece*, (1902), at 581

and of introducing other new divinities. He is also guilty of corrupting the youth. The punishment demanded is death.'[2] So there were three counts: refusing to recognize the gods recognized by the city, introducing new (or strange, *kaina*) divinities, and corrupting the youth. Adequate notice, it would seem, allowed Socrates to prepare a defence.

The Athenian process required a preliminary hearing in cases of impiety before the king archon, a magistrate charged with oversight of religious offences, in whose discretion it lay whether to forward the case to trial. His function was analogous to that of a modern judge holding a preliminary inquiry to determine whether sufficient evidence – in the Athenian process, evidence both as to fact and law – existed to warrant trial. We know from Plato's *Euthyphro* that Socrates appeared before the king in preliminary hearing and was given opportunity to answer the charges against him. The king, in forwarding the case to trial, had made a preliminary determination that the charges against Socrates, if true, tended to subvert worship in the city of Athena and, by endangering sacred custom, endangered the city itself. He had presumably also found that there was sufficient indication of their truth to warrant trial.

The trial itself was public – very public, since it took place before five hundred dicasts and a large and fractious audience. The dicasts were citizens functioning both as jurymen and judges, finding both fact and law – which law, it may be added, might be placed in evidence before them. Precautions were taken to ensure the impartiality of the tribunal. The dicasts were sworn to render judgment according to their true opinion. They were chosen by lot and assigned to their respective courts immediately before trial in order to prevent tampering. The very size of their number, the fact that they were quite literally a popular court, itself had historical antecedents grounded in the quest for impartiality. Cases had once been tried by the magistrates themselves, who were members of the aristocracy. Solon, the great Athenian lawgiver of the sixth century, had introduced appeal from the decisions of magistrates to a popular court, the Heliaia, because of suspicion of class bias, and with the rapid development of democratic institutions in Athens in the fifth century, along with increased judicial business, that court of appeal was transformed into a plurality of courts of first instance. This history, in part at least, helps to explain what is otherwise difficult to understand, namely, that there was no appeal from the decision of an Athenian court in a criminal case in 399 BC.

---

2 Diogenes Laertius II.40. Translation here and elsewhere by the author unless otherwise noted

When you had had your trial you had had your appeal, after the preliminary finding of the magistrate.

The trial itself was an adversary proceeding. Greek vocabulary on this point is interesting: the accuser was 'the pursuer' and the accused 'the fleer,' metaphors which closely match our 'prosecutor' and 'defendant'; the trial itself was an *agon tes dikes*, a contest of right. Socrates and his accusers were given equal time, measured by a water-clock, to make their statements to the court. The rules of evidence were laxly enforced, as one might expect in a court of five hundred judges, but rules there were. The accuser could be cross-examined and witnesses summoned both by prosecution and defence. Law could be entered in evidence (with threat of the death penalty for those who cited non-existent law). Requirements of relevance were loose and seem to have been served, in criminal cases, mainly by the water-clock; you could say pretty much what you pleased, but you had a strictly limited amount of time in which to say it. Still, certain types of hearsay were, in theory at least, excluded, and perjury punished. There was no burden of proof, or more accurately, persuasion, nor any institutionalized analogue thereof: conviction was obtained by the vote of a simple majority, with acquittal in case of a tie. The prosecutor was fined, however, if he did not obtain a fifth part of the vote, a step taken to inhibit malicious prosecution. At this date, at least, parties to a criminal action appear to have been required to plead in person, not by attorney,[3] and rhetoric thus became a skill that many of the more well-to-do citizens found it advisable to acquire: but there were rhetors, experts both in law and oratory, whom you could hire to brief your case and, indeed, write your speech for you. There is a tradition that Lysias, one of the best of them, offered to brief Socrates, but that Socrates refused.

Socrates therefore had notice and an opportunity to be heard before a tribunal meant to be impartial. In a descriptive sense of due process, he was found guilty according to due process of law. Still, there is a feature in the brief portrait of the Athenian trial process I have just drawn that is worth remarking. It is that law was pleaded in evidence. The late A.R.W. Harrison, a distinguished student of Athenian law, wrote:[4]

We may find it strange that laws and decrees should be classed as evidence; we regard evidence as directed towards establishing the facts, while laws and decrees constitute the framework of rules under which the facts have to be subsumed. But in

---

3 Cf Plato, *Apology* 19a.
4 *The Laws of Athens: Procedure* (1971), at 134

the Athenian courts of the fourth century there was no sharp distinction between decisions on law and on facts. Both were ultimately in the hands of the dikasts, and there was no judge experienced in the law whose task it was, with the help of advocates likewise experienced, to explicate the rules (of which laws would be the leading constituent) which should govern the decision on the facts. It was inevitable therefore that the litigant should have the duty of laying before the court any law or decree relevant to his case, whether he were plaintiff or defendant, and that the laws thus cited should come to be regarded as on all fours with evidence in convincing the dikasts to vote in his favour.

Bentham long ago condemned the arcane technicalities of 'Judge & Co.' and urged that law should be 'cognoscible.' But there is a distinction, after all, between legal underbrush and a benign technicality aimed at precision. Athenian law, at the trial stage at least, was magnificently untechnical and eminently cognoscible to the lay intelligence. The result was to substitute rhetoric and persuasion for proof and to open the door wide to the evils of vagueness.

Notice the effect of all this on a finding of legal guilt. A verdict, it will be said, contains a factual component: it is either true to fact or false. But what is meant by a 'fact'?

Take Jones and his burglary. Blackstone defines burglary as a breaking and entering of any dwelling-house by night with intent to commit felony, and he also defines those elements; the precision of his account is further protected by the principle that criminal law is to be construed strictly, so that what is not clearly within the definition is outside it. When Jones is charged with burglary and brought to trial, the court faces a direct empirical question to be settled by evidence, namely, Did he do it? A verdict of guilty is the answer: Yes, he did.

But then, the question 'Did he do it?' presupposes that we know with some precision what 'it' is. A verdict involves not only a statement of fact but also a legal classification of fact, that is, a classification of fact according to rules of law. If we are to impute burglary to Jones, we must find that he did given acts and that those acts are of a kind subsumed under the rule forbidding burglary. Being found in a dwelling-house by night is relevant; needing a shave and a haircut is not. A legal system that does not provide clear definition of the elements that go to constitute offences will be characterized, in practice, by implicit and unannounced retroactivity; it will allow new elements to be imported into an offence – into a writ, given a formulary system of the kind that obtained in Athens – elements that do not provide an acknowledged and prospective basis for the charge. This sort of retroactivity does not arise from the retrospective application of a clearly defined rule; it arises from the apparently and deceptively prospective application of an unclearly defined rule, a rule whose elements are unsettled at the circumference. It is basically a kind of vagueness; and because it will serve not only to convict those who have had no prospective reason to expect a charge but also to deter those who find themselves without basis for predicting when they may attract a charge, it involves a type of overbreadth that is in two ways destructive of liberty. Given a developed principle of stare decisis (i.e. following precedent), this sort of vagueness can be cured, piece by piece and bit by bit, after the fact; retrospective delineation of the contours of an offence will in the long run yield considerable clarity of definition. Nor does this sort of retrospectivity sin against legality, so long as it consists in expanding a rule to the reach of its *proximate* reason, for it is the reason, not the technical expression of the rule, that is in general understood by those to whom the law is directed. But the Athenian system was unbound, except persuasively, by precedent: the elements of impiety were what a simple majority of the dicasts on any given day thought was impious. There was no cure, not even after the fact, and the reasons a jury might entertain could be as broad as 'general social welfare' – or social prejudice.

Unsettled elements may at least allow of proof according to empirical standards of fact. It is otherwise when the elements themselves are undefined, when they are vague and lacking any clear standard of application. The trier of fact is then left at large in determining what kind of fact he is supposed to try, and the very notion that verdicts contain a factual component will require some modification. A trial is a search for truth. But what kind of truth? When the search is no longer restricted to determining whether given acts satisfy determinate conditions for application of a rule, it will inevitably enlarge into questions about what may loosely be called 'conduct,' about the character of the man you are dealing with, and whether you approve or disapprove of him. That is, questions of guilt or innocence will come to be settled, not on the basis of what he did – or did not do – but on the basis of what kind of man you think he is.

Facts, in short, are a function of the legal rules by which they are classified, and if those rules are vague and ill-defined, the facticity of facts, so to speak, will be commensurately affected. And since proof is a function of fact, degeneration of fact-requirements will lead to degeneration of proof-requirements. Trials we may still have; but their outcome will turn on rhetoric and persuasion – specifically, persuasion about what a fine fellow you are and what a nasty fellow your opponent is – rather than on empirically ascertainable standards of proof. This description matches the actual course of Greek pleading, as may be verified from Aristotle's *Rhetoric*. Indeed, what we should be inclined to call rules of evidence are there discussed under the heading of rules of persuasion.[5]

Return, then, to the claim that, though in equity Socrates was innocent, he was guilty in Athenian law. Guilty by what standards of guilt? The answer, I think, is guilty by no standards at all, except the formal standard of having been voted guilty. Socrates died, not because of what he did, but because he was the sort of man he was. His trial was in effect a political trial, and the fact that it could have taken place as it did constitutes a severe indictment of the legal quality of Athenian law.[6] Samuel Eliot Morison, the distinguished American historian, once remarked that a legal system must in the long run be judged by the extremes it will tolerate. We deal here with an extreme.

Impiety, no doubt, was a serious matter. A sign of this was that it was prosecuted by *graphe*, or writ of public indictment, as technically even murder was not, because it directly affected the welfare and safety of the city as a whole. As Euthyphro puts it, 'The opposite of what is acceptable to the gods is impious, and impiety overturns and destroys all things.'[7] To leave impiety unpunished was to invite divine retribution, and in the year 399 BC, five years after ruinous defeat in war and the rise and overthrow of a murderous oligarchy, the Thirty Tyrants, Athens must have felt that the hand of God had already lain heavy upon her.

Still, impiety lay generally for a reasonably well-defined class of wrongs: for temple-theft, for profanation of the Eleusinian Mysteries, for mutilation

5 *Rhetoric* I.xv

6 James Madison, in Number 10 of the *Federalist*, gave a concise and accurate diagnosis of what had gone wrong:

'A pure democracy, by which I mean a society consisting of a small number of citizens, who assemble and administer the government in person, can admit of no cure from the mischiefs of faction. A common passion or interest will, in almost every case, be felt by a majority of the whole; a communication and concert, results from the form of government itself; and there is nothing to check the inducements to sacrifice the weaker party, or an obnoxious individual. Hence it is, that such democracies have ever been spectacles of turbulence and contention; have ever been found incompatible with personal security, or the rights of property; and have, in general, been as short in their lives, as they have been violent in their deaths.'

Madison, it may be observed, was a close student of ancient constitutions, and this is a remarkably precise description of the failure of the Athenian polity, of which the trial of Socrates stands as a vivid symbol.

7 *Euthyphro* 14b

of sacred objects, for blasphemy or sacrilege affecting the religion and worship of the state. It did not, in general, lie for unorthodoxy in belief; Athens was singularly free of the unlovely habit of persecuting men for their opinions. Athenian religion was a matter, not of dogma, but of ritual observance – of *dromena*, things done, rather than of *legomena*, things said. Issues of orthodoxy or heterodoxy had little bearing – appropriately enough, given a polytheistic religion whose credal content, if so it may be called, was largely supplied by the myths of Homer and Hesiod. Impiety, in short, lay normally for definite kinds of act.

The reach of the writ of impiety had been extended by the prosecution of the philosopher Anaxagoras, some thirty or forty years earlier. Anaxagoras was tried, fined, and exiled from Athens for saying that Sun was stone and the Moon earth, and (by implication) not the gods they were traditionally supposed to be. But that trial had been politically inspired, as an indirect way of striking at Pericles through his friends, and it appears to have required special legislation to bring the case into court under the writ. In any event, Socrates did not teach what Anaxagoras taught,[8] and there is indeed no evidence that he taught at all about religious matters, though there is evidence enough that he often asked questions, embarrassing to zealots, about the details of Olympian theology. Socrates had walked his peculiar way for many years without attracting a charge, and this could not have been so if his conduct fell within any clearly defined standard of wrong.

If Socrates' speech of defence is accurately represented in Plato's *Apology*, it is a highly peculiar statement. Importantly, it does not deny the charges against him.

Socrates meets the charge of irreligion by cross-examining Meletus, his accuser, and trapping him in inconsistency. Meletus had been incautious enough to assert that Socrates believed in no gods at all, that he was a complete atheist, while yet alleging in his indictment the introduction of new divinities. Socrates merely shows that since divinities are either gods or children of gods, recognition of divinities implies recognition of gods. He later denies atheism in stated terms; but he does not deny the charge of not acknowledging the gods the city acknowledges. Everything we know of him indicates that his worship was both orthodox and sincere – but then, along with many of his fellow-citizens, he doubted some of the myths. Again, he nowhere denies the charge of introducing new divinities; he only explains the charge by reference to his Sign, a kind of voice that came to

8 See *Apology* 28d-e.

him at times and held him back from what he was about to do and which he explicitly describes as god-like and divine. Not once does he deny impiety as such.

But the heart of the charges, to judge both from what we know of Socrates and from the controversy about the trial afterwards, was not irreligion but corrupting the youth. Hyperides, a younger contemporary of Plato born a decade after the trial, remarked that 'our ancestors punished Socrates for what he said (*epi logois*).'[9] This is true, but the truth did not stand and work alone. Fifty years after the trial, Aeschines suggested that Athens had put Socrates to death because he had been a teacher of Critias, one of the Thirty Tyrants;[10] it may be added that Charmides, also a member of the Socratic circle in early life, was among that unholy number.[11] Still another member of Socrates' circle was the brilliant Alcibiades, who turned traitor to Athens during the Peloponnesian War. The sophist Polycrates cited the latter as an example in his 'Accusation of Socrates,' a set-speech written in or shortly after 393 BC which the rhetorician Isocrates roundly condemned in the *Busiris* as bad rhetoric.[12]

We do not have Meletus' speech of accusation or the supporting speeches of Anytus and Lycon. The names of Critias, Charmides, and Alcibiades may not have been so much as directly mentioned, for the terms of the amnesty proclaimed when the democracy was restored after the overthrow of the Thirty forbade such testimony – though that did not prevent it from becoming commonplace in the law courts. But the charge of corrupting the youth would have been without effect[13] had Meletus and those around him not been able to count on the appropriate examples springing quickly and nimbly to mind. Thus, although Socrates' own conduct under the Thirty was heroic[14] and widely known, he was tied to them, and to a brilliant traitor, in remembered association.

The charge of corrupting the youth was important, indeed crucial; yet

---

9 Frag. 55 (Kenyon)

10 *In Timarchus* 173

11 The Thirty came to power in the summer of 404 BC after a reaction at the end of the Peloponnesian War, which the radical democracy was widely blamed for losing. Welcomed at first, they brought a reign of terror which lasted some eight months until they were overthrown. Critias and Charmides were not only members of the Socratic circle but also kinsmen of Plato, whose judgment of them may be inferred from ? *Epistle VII* 324b–325a. For further discussion see Hignett, *History of the Athenian Constitution*, (1967), at chap. 11 and appendices 13 and 14.

12 *Busiris*, paras 5–6 (Van Hook)

13 Cf *Apology* 33d–34a.

14 See *Apology* 32c–d.

Socrates never directly denies it. He argues against Meletus that *either* he does not corrupt the youth *or* he corrupts them unintentionally – but, issues of *mens rea* apart, this is not to deny that he corrupts them. He lists a goodly number of witnesses who will testify on the point in his behalf – and suggests that Meletus call them. He denies that he corrupts by teaching on the ground that he has never taught or taken money for it; but he admits that it is open to anyone to hear what he has to say. The closest he comes to denying the charge itself is to describe his peculiar mission to Athens – that of urging men to pursue virtue – adding, '*If* in saying these things I corrupt the youth, that would be harm indeed.'[15]

In his speech of defence Socrates therefore does not deny the charges against him. And there is more.

In diction and structure, Socrates' speech is rhetorical. The bulk of his argument is directed, not towards Meletus and the formal indictment, but towards the prejudice raised against him by 'the old accusers,' especially Aristophanes in *The Clouds*, first produced over twenty years earlier. Socrates suggests that the charge of impiety gained credence from the fact that he was confused in the popular mind with the sophists. Aristophanes portrayed him as a man who inquired into things in the heavens and beneath the earth, and made the weaker argument stronger, and, as Socrates says, 'the men who spread that report are my dangerous accusers, for their hearers think that those who inquire into such things acknowledge no gods.'[16] The charge of making the weaker argument stronger – Wrong Logic triumphs over Right Logic in *The Clouds* – was particularly damaging, carrying with it the implication of sophistry and pernicious scepticism.

But the sophists' stock in trade was rhetoric. Since Socrates was identified with the sophists, and this was a serious matter of complaint, true rhetoric would require that he abstain from anything even resembling rhetoric. Had he chosen to conduct his defence in plain speech, he would have done much to allay the prejudice against him. Instead, he disclaims ability to speak in the course of a masterful speech before an audience throughly familiar with the uses of political and forensic oratory. His hearers could scarcely have found the apparent attempt at deception endearing. Thus, although Socrates denies, point by point, the portrait offered of him in *The Clouds*, his use of rhetoric suggested sophistry, and the very skill of his use confirmed the suggestion. His substantive denials, though true, were made to seem false by the manner in which they were

15 *Apology* 30a–b; cf *Euthyphro* 2c–3a.
16 *Apology* 18c

issued. In circumstances that called for appearing as an ordinary, domesticated, farm-yard fowl, Socrates gave himself the character of the fox.

As Aristotle remarks, one rule of forensic pleading is to make your character look right; this Socrates does not do. Another rule is to put your audience in the right frame of mind: 'When people are feeling friendly and placable, they think one sort of thing; when they are feeling angry or hostile, they think either something totally different or the same thing with a different intensity; when they feel friendly to the man who comes before them for judgement, they regard him as having done little wrong, if any; when they feel hostile, they take the opposite view.'[17] This is an illuminating comment on the workings of a Greek court, and perhaps of any jury; but since this jury also sat as judges, it implies much about the relative role of persuasion as against proof. Clearly, if you mean to persuade, it is best not to offend, and the advice becomes more urgent if you are pleading a cause before five hundred dicasts who will find both fact and law and who will be moved, humanly, quite as much by their emotions as their intellects.

Socrates does little enough to make his dicasts feel 'friendly and placable.' The manner in which he deals with the counterpenalty stands as a symbol of the speech of defence itself. He has been found guilty. Meletus has proposed death. Socrates must suggest an alternate penalty, and between those two penalties the court, by law, must choose without alteration. At this, of all points, Socrates suggests that if penalty is to be assessed according to desert, his penalty should be public subsistence in the Prytaneum in the manner of an Olympic victor. The same tone is a constant undercurrent in his speech of defence. He disclaims clever speaking before an audience well familiar with its devices, but uses clever speech. He uses rhetoric to deny sophistry. On trial for impiety, he politely explains that the conduct that brought him there was prompted by obedience to God. He attacks politicians, poets, and craftsmen for claiming knowledge of things of which they are ignorant before a jury of five hundred men and a large and restless audience, most of whom had served in some political office, worked as craftsmen, and regarded poets as sources of moral and religious instruction. Socrates is here doing something more than telling his judges that they are a group of ignorant men. He is punching an exposed political nerve. He is telling a jury of democrats, who have sore and vivid memories of oligarchical persecution under the Thirty and genuine fear for the stability of their reconstituted democracy, that they and their leadership are

17 *Rhetoric* II.1377b 30 ff (Oxford translation)

grossly and radically ignorant.[18] He is challenging the basic piety on which government by the many rested – and his habit of so doing was a principal reason for the charge that he corrupted the youth. It is beside the point that he would have challenged with equal effect the pieties of government by the few.

This not only goes to explain why Socrates was convicted; it also explains why, in 399 BC, he was brought to trial. *The Clouds* was a source of prejudice, but it had been produced in 423. Alcibiades was an associate, but that was before the Sicilian Expedition in 415. Critias and Charmides were associates, but the Thirty had fallen early in 403. Four years, politically, is a long time, and more is required to account for the time lapse than busy courts and crowded dockets. Charges might stick through past history, but they were prompted by present offence.

The nature of that offence is exhibited in Plato's *Meno*, in a conversation between Socrates and Anytus, soon to be a witness against him and probably the moving force behind Meletus' action. It is significant that Anytus, a leader of the restored democracy, was a political moderate.[19] But his hatred of sophists runs deep, and Socrates comes very near to baiting him about it.[20] Anytus' belief that the citizens of Athens offer education in virtue – a traditional piece of democratic piety strenuously reaffirmed by Meletus in the *Apology* – is subjected to calm and merciless criticism, which cuts the more deeply for its very lightness of touch: men held to be examples of virtue cannot teach their own sons to be virtuous. How, then, can they teach others? Socrates takes as examples the democratic worthies of Athens' Golden Age – Themistocles, Pericles, and the rest – and Anytus, angered far out of proportion, accuses him of slander and issues a veiled threat. The threat is interesting: 'Beware. It may be that in other cities too it is easier to do evil to men than good. Certainly it is in

18 See also *Apology* 31e–32a, where he suggests that it is impossible for a decent man to play an active role in the politics of Athenian democracy and survive. He is speaking to a large group of survivors.

19 Though one with a mixed reputation. Aristotle in the *Constitution of Athens* (27, 4–5) criticizes Pericles' institution of jury pay as leading to deterioration of the quality of men who served on juries and goes on to remark, almost casually, 'Moreover, bribery came into existence after this, the first person to introduce it being Anytus, after his command at Pylos [in 411 BC]. He was prosecuted by certain individuals on account of his loss of Pylos, but escaped by bribing the jury' (Oxford translation). In light of this and other evidence, it is not surprising that Plato should so frequently describe Socrates' accusers as knaves.

20 *Meno* 91b–d

this one.'[21] The very intensity of Anytus' emotion, too great in the circumstances, shows how Socrates, as he describes in the *Apology*, went to the politicians and later the craftsmen and poets, questioned them, made them angry, and became hated.

Their anger, in its unreasonableness, stemmed from something more than wounded pride. The fabric of shared loyalties and beliefs that bind a people had been torn; it had been patched for five years but was very far from mended. A calm, united people can accept criticism of their institutions with tolerance and even a smile, but a people hammered apart on the anvil of events, and then regrouped, has known fear. Socrates' questioning roused memories of past danger. He touched, even in his speech of defence, the most powerful and terrible of all political motives: fear, whose image is anger. He did not walk away alive.

The reasons for finding him guilty can be put in a kind of syllogism: impiety threatens the safety of the city; Socrates threatens the safety of the city; therefore, Socrates is impious. Popular emotion, the grudging slander of the many represented in all its unreasoning intensity by Anytus, is not stayed in its course by logic. Socrates went to his death on the basis of an undistributed middle – or if you will, a middle distributed only by anger and fear.

The question arises, Why did not Socrates defend himself to better effect? The question is not a new one; it occurred, for example, to Xenophon. The answer offered by Plato's *Apology* is simple, so simple it seems complicated: Socrates' aim was neither conviction nor acquittal – the latter of which could have been won only by a type of rhetoric that amounted to abject pandering.[22] When Socrates said he could not make a speech, it was this kind of speech he meant he could not make – the kind normally expected of a defendant on trial for his life. His own aim was to tell the truth in accordance with justice, let the chips fall where they may.

Thus, for example, Socrates, wiser than other men only in knowing that he did not know, could not on the basis of knowledge deny the charges brought against him. He was indicted on a writ of impiety. But in order to know whether his conduct in cross-questioning people had been impious, it was necessary first to know what piety is. Does impiety mean urging men to pursue virtue – and convicting them of ignorance? That question cannot be answered with knowledge by a man who knows himself to be ignorant of what piety is. Nor can Socrates appeal to law for elements which constitute

21 *Meno* 94e
22 Cf *Apology* 38d–39b.

the offence of impiety: for the law is so vaguely defined as to imply that impiety is what the majority of dicasts on a given day think is impious.

As with the writ, so with the counts. A man who does not know what virtue is can deny that he intentionally corrupts the youth; but he cannot deny that he corrupts them, since knowledge of vice implies knowledge of its opposite, and he does not know what virtue is. Once again, the law helps not in framing a defence: it does not define those acts, even generically, that constitute corrupting the youth.

A man can deny that he corrupts by teaching if he has never taught but only questioned. He cannot deny that he corrupts by introducing strange divinities and not acknowledging old ones if he is himself ignorant not only in matters of virtue but also in matters of religion. Does one, or does one not, acknowledge the gods the city acknowledges if one doubts that certain stories told of them, specifically of their hatred and enmity towards one another, are true? Does one corrupt the youth by expressing those doubts? Can one, or can one not, deny the introduction of new or strange divinities, given the presence of an accustomed Sign believed to be divine? Does one corrupt the youth by mentioning the Sign? To deny such charges on the basis of knowledge, one must first understand what they mean. Again, the law is no help. It does not define those acts that will sustain a charge of introducing new divinities or of not acknowledging the gods acknowledged by the city.

Socrates' character in the *Apology* is of a piece with his character in the other early Platonic dialogues of search. Because he avowed ignorance in matters that seemed obvious to men who thought themselves wise, he seemed sly and dishonest; irony, sometimes, is in the eye of the beholder. But his ignorance was real, not feigned, and it issued in a form of inquiry that involved *elenchus*, refutation. The merit of *elenchus* was to purge the false conceit of knowledge. If it thereby chastened, it also stirred many men to wrath, and their anger was kindled higher by the appearance of wrong logic and deceit. Socrates had no wish to be hated. His service to the God caused him to be hated; and he perceived the fact with grief and pain. But he also maintained the soldier's station in which the God had placed him. Brought into court and compelled to abandon his customary form of inquiry by question and answer and to make a speech, he aimed at truth, so far as he could tell it, about his own character and his mission to Athens. He used rhetoric, for in his hands rhetoric was neither sophistry nor pandering, but an art of persuasion aimed solely at truth. The result appeared to be an astonishing arrogance. But his speech was an exhibition, not of arrogance, but of service to the God and his own mission, and of that courage, allied to wisdom, which consists in knowing when not to be afraid. He was condemned to death – condemned, not because he had broken a law, but because he had angered men and frightened them.

I earlier suggested that where the principle of legality is seriously infringed, procedural fairness is lost. If Plato's account of Socrates' speech of defence is accurate, it illustrates the point. Socrates did not deny the charges against him. He did not, I have suggested, because he could not. Quite apart from the moral and philosophical question of the real nature of piety and impiety, there was a legal difficulty; the charges provided no standard by which empirically ascertainable fact could be adduced either to support or refute them; they admitted neither proof nor disproof. Socrates was compelled to conduct his defence, not on whether he had violated a clearly formulated legal rule, but on whether he was the sort of man who was socially desirable or undesirable. That is why his speech mainly dealt, not with the formal charges brought against him under which he was nominally being tried, but with prejudice arising from informal accusations going back more than twenty years, popularly circulated, and based on ripest hearsay. He was primarily defending himself, not against an indictment, but against slander and against the fact that he was widely regarded as a threat to the established order of things. This, in practice, was what notice and an opportunity to be heard before an impartial tribunal had boiled down to.

Perhaps as just a comment on the trial of Socrates as has ever been made was offered by Karl Llewellyn in quite another context:

Angel or devil, a man has a claim to a fair trial of his guilt. Angel or devil, he has a claim to a fair trial, not of his general social desirability, but of his guilt of *the specific offense* charged against him. Such is the letter of our law. Such also is our law's spirit. For letter and for spirit there is a reason. Law is administered by men. We do not trust men to be wholly wise, or wholly fair. Above all, we do not trust men to be wise or fair to those with whose opinions, with whose interests, with whose dear-held beliefs their own interests, their own dear-held opinions, clash. 'General social desirability' of others, through most of history, has meant to men in power such attitudes and actions and opinions as do not threaten their own continuance in power ... There must be some *objective* certainty, that men can fix upon and see and prove, before we trust officialdom to act. It is too easy to find 'general' indications against one's enemies – be they Bolsheviks, or Democrats, or rivals for the Tenth Ward leadership ... The job of court and jury is to see *whether* the suspect has committed *the particular offense*. [23]

---

23 Printed for the first time in Michael and Wechsler, *Criminal Law and its Administration*, (1940), at 1086-7 (Italics Llewellyn's)

This comment, as it happens, was offered on the trial of Sacco and Vanzetti. It may serve to warn us that in the long struggle of mankind for equal justice under law, complacency is not a venial but a deadly sin, and the battle for justice is not a distant, long-won victory, but a new fight every day.

Let me now sum up. In a legal system in which rules of criminal law are so loosely defined that it is difficult to say in given cases what specific acts, if any, constitute a breach of them, innocence and guilt lose precise meaning, as does proof. Impiety in Athens had a clear centre – temple-theft, for example – but a vague circumference, so that in given cases it could only be defined at law as what a bare majority of dicasts thought to be impious. The Athenian legal system had no check on whether the decision was right: its procedure did not, and could not, cure defective substance. Indeed, it aggravated it; a procedure requiring laymen to find not only fact but law is incompatible with the technical precision required by legality.

Socrates was tried under an adversary system. But there is no single process properly called *the* adversary system, and the Athenian version, by failing to adhere to the principle of legality, substituted persuasion for proof and condemnation for guilt. The adversary system at common law, with all its flaws, is a different thing. It involves more than people fighting each other in a courtroom or even fighting each other according to rule. It involves the strenuous assertion of rights claimed under principles of legal rationality, of which legality and procedural fairness are essential parts, as a bulwark against the exercise of arbitrary power. As Aristotle put it long ago: 'To invest the law with authority is, it seems, to invest God and reason only; to invest a man is to introduce a beast, as desire is something bestial, and even the best of men in authority are liable to be corrupted by passion. We may conclude that law is reason without passion and it is preferable to any individual.'[24] To a degree that Aristotle did not and could not realize, the reason he extolled was what Coke once called, in a memorable interview with James I, 'the artificial reason and judgement of the law,'[25] 'artificial,' not as feigned or fictitious, but as proceeding according to rules of art, rules aimed at proof, at fact, at legality, at procedural fairness. It is that artifact which gives content to the ancient ideal of a government of laws, not men, and to the inestimable good of liberty under law.

It is easy to take for granted what is familiar. It is also easy to lose what is taken for granted. The values of legality and procedural fairness, and the constitutional and other limitations that give those values working force,

24 *Politics* III.1287a.28–32 (Welldon translation)
25 For the interview see (1609), 7 Co. *Rep.* 63–5.

should, it seems to me, be kept clearly and steadily before the mind in any discussion of law reform. Ideas have a determining role in history; what men believe shapes what they do, and if their beliefs are ill-informed or ill-thought through, their best and noblest intentions will often be productive of evils. Mr Justice Brandeis, dissenting in *Olmstead*, observed that 'Experience should teach us to be most on our guard to protect liberty when the Government's purposes are beneficent. Men born to freedom are naturally alert to repel invasion of their liberty by evil-minded rulers. The greatest dangers to liberty lurk in insidious encroachment by men of zeal, well-meaning but without understanding.'[26] In a similar vein, Professor Lon Fuller has written about certain suggested reforms in the criminal law:

> I have spoken of 'noble' impulses as having played a part in confusing the concept of responsibility. An outstanding example lies in abuses of the rehabilitative ideal in the criminal law. As Francis Allen has demonstrated, misapplied, this ideal can brutalize the criminal law it sought to make more humane. When, for example, rehabilitation is taken as the exclusive aim of the criminal law, all concern about due process and a clear definition of what is criminal may be lost. If the worst that can happen to the defendant is that he should be given a chance to have himself improved at public expense, why all the worry about a fair trial?[27]

Both Brandeis and Fuller are concerned with apparent goods purchased at the cost of legality. Fuller, indeed, suggests that where procedural fairness and the principle of legality are at issue, there, if anywhere, there is need for the institution of judicial review.

A concluding remark on jurisprudence. It is possible to say that Athenian law and common law are both law. But if law is, as Professor Fuller suggests, an enterprise of subjecting human conduct to the governance of rules, it is also possible to say that Athenian law, because of its inadequate institutionalization of the principle of legality and procedural fairness, fell short of lawfulness, that in operation it was too often a specimen of lawless law. There are those who will find in the notion of 'lawless law' a contradiction in terms; I submit that it describes a fact of everyday occurrence. Law is not morals. Indeed, one of the things wrong with Athenian law was too large an injection of the loose and emotive standards of popular morality. But it is worth asking, with Fuller, whether there is not an inner morality of law itself, and whether legality and procedural fairness are not essential

26 *Olmstead* v *U.S.*, (1927), 277 U.S. 438 at 479
27 *The Morality of Law* (2d ed, 1969) at 165

elements of it. No doubt, as Professor Hart has argued,[28] those elements are unfortunately compatible with very great iniquity. Yet, with them, even a slave under a slave code is guaranteed important rights. It is surely reasonable to hold that where those rights are denied, there is denial of law, and law that countenances such denial is, by so much, law that falls short of its own inner aim, falls short of what it is to be law.

REGINALD ALLEN is a professor in the Department of Philosophy, University of Toronto, and teaches courses in jurisprudence in that department and at the Faculty of Law. He has taught at a number of American universities, including Yale, where he received his PH D. A contributor to various philosophical and classical journals, and author of books on Plato, he is at present on leave at the Institute for Advanced Study at Princeton.

28 H.L.A. Hart, *The Concept of Law* (1961), at 202

ANATOL RAPOPORT

Theories of conflict resolution and the law

Conceptions of law and of conflict resolution are linked naturally in ideas about the origin of law, at least in the ideas prevalent in societies with liberal traditions, according to which laws came into being in the process of codifying rules of accepted conduct; these, in turn, evolved in response to the needs for reducing the level of internal violence in societies. This conception of law rests on several implicit assumptions that I should like to re-examine and therefore must make explicit.

A first assumption is that there exist entities called 'societies,' essentially organizational frameworks, which provide individuals with opportunities to engage in mutually rewarding collaboration and co-operation. For these co-operative processes to function smoothly, conflicts among the constituent individuals or groups must be avoided, alleviated, or resolved, and deviant behaviour discouraged. Next, an assumption underlying the social philosophies derived from liberal traditions concerns the existence of 'natural rights,' meaning certain prerogatives with which a human individual comes into the world. Societies (or at least their governments) are conceived as having been invented to guarantee these prerogatives to individuals. For instance, if each individual has a natural right to 'life,' society, through its laws, must protect that right by guiding conflicts among individuals away from paths leading to personal violence, and so on. Finally, it is assumed that specific institutional arrangements result from consensus among 'free contracting parties' and are therefore subject to change in accordance with the changing needs or experiences of the constituents.

Essentially, this describes the liberal creed. Much of it is spelled out in documents such as underwrote the founding of the American republic. Acceptance of this creed induces also an understandable reverence for The Law as, if not the absolute, nonetheless the ultimate, arbiter of right and wrong in social conduct. Hence the law functions not only as a resolver of interpersonal or intergroup conflicts but also of intrapersonal conflict engendered by clashing imperatives. I am sure that in the days of slavery in the United States, for instance, there were many law enforcement officers having strong personal aversions to slavery who nevertheless submissively arrested fugitive slaves to be returned to 'legal' masters, feeling the satisfaction, however bitter, of having done their duty to society.

Of course, the 'liberal' conception of law is not the only one, either historically or geographically. Two others come to mind. One is the ecclesiastical conception according to which secular laws reflect, or are supposed to reflect, immutable divine law, which stems, not from particular organizational needs of human societies, but from the will of God. Another is the Marxist. Though the latter is actually a conception of the state rather than of law specifically, since the state operates for the most part through law it is not improper to speak of the Marxist theory of law. I should like to discuss some of its aspects because they are relevant to what I shall have to say later.

Marx's ideas about the origin of human societies are different from those on which the liberal creed is based. The innately free individual coming in contact with other equally free individuals for purposes of trade or for establishing a 'social contract' is absent in the Marxist approach. Man is considered to have been social even before he became man, so that there was no question of any rationally conceived 'purpose' to form an organized society, much less a government. The social unit was originally a biological unit held together by gregarious instincts that had evolved in consequence of their survival value. It is supposed that social differentiation arose as a result of division of labour, which, in turn, followed the elaboration of technology. And it is this social differentiation rather than social cohesion engendered by 'the needs of society' that, according to Marx, plays the part of the prime mover in social dynamics and evolution.

Thus, in Marx's theory society appears, not as a harmonious whole with needs defined as some totality of the needs of the individuals comprising it, these needs being served by the institutions, including law, but rather as an arena of constant struggle in which now one, now another, newly emerging social class becomes dominant. As a social class becomes dominant it organizes the institutions, including the legal system, in accordance with its class needs, the principal of these needs being that of preserving its dominant position.

The state, in the Marxist conception, is an instrument by which the dominance of a social class is maintained and hence is essentially an instrument of oppression; by implication, so are the laws by means of which the state imposes its authority.

It is easy to oversimplify this theory into a crude dogma that assigns an exclusively oppressive role to all functions of the state in all its forms and, consequently, to all laws governing class-differentiated societies. It is equally easy to demonstrate the sterility of such a dogma. Nevertheless, the theory, if not its vulgarized version, deserves to be taken seriously, and there have been serious attempts to refute it by presenting evidence against its basic tenet, the class origin of all the important conflicts in organized societies with differentiated structures.

One argument against the Marxist conception of social conflicts, heard with special frequency in the United States, is based on the observation that conflicts in American society are generated, not by incompatibilities of fixed class interests, but by clashes of the special interests of many diverse groups. These interests are ad hoc and shifting, as are the compositions of the groups. Consequently, there are frequent realignments and shifts of coalitions. Moreover, many individuals find themselves members simultaneously of different interest groups. This criss-crossing and flexibility of the interfaces of oppositions, it is maintained, prevents the crystallization of a sharp class struggle of the sort envisaged by Marx and casts doubt on the idea of the state, hence of its legal system, being the guardian of particular class interests. Instead, the state is perceived as a sort of referee, seeing to it that the conflicts generated by diverse interests are conducted within acceptable bounds without disrupting the functioning of 'society,' whose organic nature and beneficent nurturing role is thereby implicitly asserted. The argument can be supported by ample evidence; for example, legislation successfully sponsored by organized labour, whereby the interests of the working class rather than the bourgeoisie is supposedly served, despite the latter being supposedly the dominant class in all capitalist societies.

The counterargument on this point often advanced by Marxists is that legislation favouring labour serves the purpose of diluting the class consciousness of the working class and so in the long run serves to preserve the capitalist system. Admittedly, the facts are consistent with both hypotheses: that the state is neutral and that the laws serve to diffuse intrasocial conflict in the interest of 'society as a whole,' and that the state is the instrument of the dominant class, 'the bourgeoisie,' which uses this instrument even to limit its own power when necessary to preserve the system that guarantees its dominant position.

At this point, an 'ideologically neutral' social scientist might suggest an objective scientific test to decide between the two hypotheses. One could select a 'random sample' of laws or legal decisions. Further, one could choose some objective criterion whereby the elements of that sample could be judged as being more advantageous to one or the other class. Finally, one could apply statistical procedures to test the hypothesis that legislative acts or legal decisions tended to favour one class more than another.

This is the 'positivist approach' to social theory – an approach which is often ascribed by Marxists to bourgeois ideology. We shall come back to this matter, but for the present I shall only point out that both the refutation by counterexamples and the proposed statistical test of Marxist theory of law miss what I believe to be the main point of the theory – that the dominant class imposes its ideology, including a value system, on the *entire* society. This is not a proposition in the 'positivist mode.' It cannot be tested by straightforward analysis of routinely gathered data. To make sense of this proposition, we must look for the 'principal theme' of a society, a creed which, even if stated in relatively few words, can impart meaning to conceptions of right and wrong, rights and obligations, justice and injustice, prevalent in that society. If one is interested in testing the Marxist theory of law, one should see whether the outlook inherent in a legal system justifies the position of the dominant social class.

My interpretation here may seem to some (primarily, I suppose, to anti-Marxists) to be a defence of Marxist philosophy at least; to others (primarily orthodox Marxists), a distortion of the doctrine. On my part, I have no axe to grind. I am firmly convinced that the most valuable contribution made by Marxist philosophy of society was its emphasis on the massive effects of social dynamics upon individual consciousness, the insistence that it is the *systemic* properties of social relations that determine the ideational content of human existence, including ideas of justice and legitimacy, rather than the other way around, as appears in the traditional liberal view of social institutions. In this way, Marx's insight is akin to that of Freud, who also emphasized the primary role of the subconscious in shaping behavioural predispositions and personality traits, that is, the influence of the 'systemic' upon the 'rational.'

At the same time, I freely admit that the nature of these subconscious prime movers, on either the individual or societal level, may not be what either Freud or Marx imagined them to be. For example, I have strong doubts about the ubiquitous importance of Oedipal fixations as generators of neuroses. Likewise, I doubt whether all forms of class exploitation can be reduced to the sort that characterize division of labour and unequal distribution of goods. (This is why my 'defence' of Marxist ideas may appear as distortions to orthodox Marxists.) I am even more impatient with attempts to reduce the Marxist theory of class exploitation to a mere tautology – 'If it cannot be shown to be rooted in relations inherent in the mode of production, it is not class exploitation.' For well-known political reasons, the Marxist theory of class exploitation was stopped in its tracks and did not advance (except in the form of 'heresies') beyond its original scope formulated a century ago. Released from theological and bureaucratic shackles, Marxist theory may yet have much to say.

And so, I abstract what I believe to be the most valuable of Marx's contributions: the recognition of the necessity to trace people's social consciousness (i.e. their value systems) to the underlying systemic, or what Marxists call 'objective,' relations between social classes and, in particular, to the specific factors from which the presently dominant class derives (or, I would add, once derived) its strength.

The relation between the dominant outlook of a society and the source of strength of its dominant class is most clear in the United States. This seems paradoxical at first thought because class differentiation seems to be less sharp and the so-called class struggle less pronounced in the United States than in any other major capitalist society. But this only means, to my way of thinking, that the imposition of the value system of the dominant class upon the other social strata has been more pervasive in the United States than elsewhere.

The dominant social class in the United States is the business class, and the keystone of its bastion of power is an idea called free enterprise or, equivalently, free competition. I shall try to show that this idea is reflected in an important aspect of the American legal system.[1] Before I pass to this main theme, I must somehow justify the statements just made, since both can be challenged.

First, in the 'multicentral' model of power relations in American society, it appears that there is no such thing as the interest of 'business.'

1 Here I should, perhaps, make an apology to Canadian readers for illustrating my arguments by references only to the United States legal system. It happens to be the only legal system with which I am somewhat familiar. Whether it applies also to the Canadian legal system I will leave to the reader to judge. If it does, then read 'American' as 'North American.'

There are interests of many business aggregates and of many other aggregates besides (labour, professional, ethnic, etc), so that it appears senseless to say that the 'business class' is dominant. Further, 'free enterprise,' however useful it may be as a rallying slogan, has undergone tremendous changes, so that the dynamics of the American economy today scarcely resemble those of incipient industrial capitalism when 'free enterprise' was more literally what it was pictured to be.

To the second objection, my reply is that it is not the 'fact' but merely the idea of 'free enterprise' that is the keystone of dominant American values; and to the extent that these values still find articulate expression, they are still couched in terms of that phrase or its equivalents: the worth and dignity of the individual reside in his liberty to 'pursue happiness,' that is, 'success,' which is manifested most typically and recognizably as business success. My answer to the first objection, related to the multiplicity of interests and power centres in American society, is that the keynote is to be sought, not in specific ad hoc advantages to be gained, but in the modus operandi 'accepted by all,' that is, the 'rules of the game.' This is no less true even if 'accepted' must be put in quotes, that is, even if acceptance reflects little more than lip service, because people pay lip service to that which they *believe* is commonly accepted, even if it is not. Belief in common acceptance is at times as good a means of social cohesion as actual acceptance. Now, 'free enterprise,' being certainly that part of the mechanism of the process whereby the American business class became immensely rich, can be said to have summarized a class interest at least in the incipient period. The fact that the principle is accepted (or paid lip service to) by most labour leaders, professionals, and so on speaks for the ideological hegemony, hence the dominance, of the business class.

The aspect of the American legal system procedure to which I want to relate the ideology of free enterprise is the so-called adversary system, in which every legal procedure is viewed as a contest between two parties (one of which may be the state) and each side is represented by spokesmen who are, in effect, responsible only for defending the interests they respectively represent. Formally or legally speaking, mention is usually made of other responsibilities. For instance, in criminal proceedings the defence attorneys no less than the prosecutors are considered as 'officers of the court,' the court being viewed as an instrument for dispensing justice. In practice, however, these responsibilities turn out to be little more than obligations to adhere to the rules of the game. Such obligations are assumed also by opposing teams in competitive sports, by participants in duels, and, in the heydays of institutionalized warfare, by belligerents. The 'game' itself is usually, though not always, conceived as a zero-sum game, where any gain by one side is balanced by a corresponding loss on the other.[2]

Logically, the adversary system leaves no room for the concept of justice. In its purest form, it would be represented by a combat between two champions, such as the combat between Lohengrin and Telramund, the outcome of which was expected to provide the verdict on the question of whether Elsa murdered her brother. Of course, even there, the link to 'justice' is made via the expectation of divine intervention on the side of truth. But once this questionable connection is left out of consideration, the combat becomes a combat pure and simple, a reduction of right to might.

It does not stretch the imagination too far to picture the adversary system as a modern version of the combat of champions. Naturally, the procedure is linked to the administration of justice – but without recourse to expected supernatural intervention. Each side is supposed to gather and present evidence relative to the facts of the case, each side being responsible for presenting evidence favouring the interest it represents. Instead of the deity, there is a jury, initially ignorant of the relative justness of those interests (unlike the deity, who knows the answer from the start) but convinced in the course of the proceedings. Still, there is no escaping the fact that the relative 'might' of the two sides plays a major part in determining the outcome. The very circumstance that cases are supposed to be decided on the weight of factual evidence emphasizes the importance of the relative power of the adversaries. In important cases, the bulk of 'relevant' evidence is often enormous. Accordingly, it takes enormous resources of time, effort, and money to gather it. The amount of effort that each side can give to amassing such evidence naturally varies in proportion to the resources available.

Available resources include more than time and costs of routine investigations. Laws, especially those involving complex property and commercial relations, are correspondingly complex and subject to interpretations varying with specific cases, and among the responsibilities of opposing representing counsels is that of pin-pointing the aspects of a case that merit an interpretation of the law favourable to the corresponding side. The ability to do this successfully depends on intricate knowledge, not only of the statutory law itself but – what is often more important – of relevant

2 For a description of game theory, see Luce and Raiffa, *Games and Decisions* (1957) and Rapoport, *Two-Person Game Theory* (1966). For an application of some of the concepts of game theory to law, see Heymann, 'The Problem of Coordination: Bargaining and Rules,' (1973), 86 *Harv. L. Rev.* 797, and Birmingham, 'Legal and Moral Duty in Game Theory: Common Law Contract and Chinese Analogies,' (1968–9) 18 *Buff. L. Rev.* 99.

precedent decisions tending to support the interpretation advanced. Such knowledge, in the form of expertise in finding and persuasively applying appropriate precedents, is itself a form of resource usually available only for sufficient monetary consideration. There is nothing surprising, then, in the well-known, openly admitted, and, on the whole, accepted fact that one's fate in the court room, whether as the accused or as a party in a civil suit, depends to a considerable extent on the amount of financial support one can muster. I do not mean to say that this fact is accepted without reservations; still, the reservations usually do not go beyond a vague regret at the way the world of affairs is structured. By the same token, it is generally conceded that the small, independent businessman can hardly hope to compete successfully against large, powerful combines, and it is proper to express regrets on that account. But the regret is an expression of sympathy (similar to that felt by the sensitive toward the losers in any contest), not of outrage.

In short, the adversary system of legal procedure faithfully reflects many aspects of the ethos that attends the 'free enterprise' conception of social justice. It reflects the primacy of competition as a guarantee of a priori social equality. If no a priori criteria of social privilege (e.g. criteria based on birth) are admissible and if 'justice' is conceived as a form of goods to be distributed like any other scarce commodity, then competition provides the needed a posteriori criterion of deserts – the better man wins. The better man proves himself by bringing fuller resources, or greater energy, or more artful astuteness to bear on the outcome of the case. It is as if the 'invisible hand,' often invoked as the justification of the market economy, is implicitly conjured to justify a similar mechanism in the administration of justice.[3] The principle assumed is that when a multitude of free individuals seek their enlightened individual interests, the total interest of society is served most efficiently. The adversary system is a direct transplant of competitive economics into the apparatus of justice.

The analogy with business competition extends beyond the court room. Law is a career like any other profession, and in a competitive society objective criteria of competitive success are highly valued. Consequently, in practically any field of endeavour, such 'objective' (usually quantitative) indices of achievement are continually calculated. They provide the competitors with measures of self-esteem and with targets of future achievement. They also provide the 'consumers' with easy-to-grasp criteria of excellence. Just as sales volumes are frequently included as selling points

3 See Weiler, 'Two Models of Judicial Decision-Making,' (1968), 46 *Can. Bar Rev.* 406, at 415.

in advertisements for consumer commodities, and attendance at theatres, popularity ratings of politicians, scores achieved by individual athletes and competitive sports teams, prices paid for works of art, serve the same purpose, a measure of legal competence is the percentage of cases won. In fact, the competence of a prosecutor as a public servant is not infrequently expressed in terms of the percentage of convictions obtained. It goes without saying that these indices exert a pressure on attorneys to choose cases likely to be won. Perhaps it is an oversimplification to say that only numbers matter to practising lawyers. It may be that winning a long shot or an especially difficult case or a case against an opposition with formidable resources is given a correspondingly large weight. And, of course, some advantages accrue even from lost causes. But such exceptions do not invalidate the analogy. (Business enterprises also engage in operations entailing losses for purposes of publicity or good will or even from a sense of public duty.)

On the whole, the impression cannot be escaped that the goal of 'serving justice' becomes at best a hoped-for by-product of typical competitive activity involving mobilization of resources, technical expertise, and ingenuity – activity that does not depend on any conception of justice or any devotion to it except, perhaps, incidentally as extra motivation. The fact that in principle an attorney-at-law is available to serve any legitimate interest and on many occasions finds himself serving on opposite sides in very similar cases makes for a powerful argument that justice is not necessarily served by extending the practices of the business world to the operation of the legal system.

There is an obvious rejoinder to this challenge: What is the alternative? The same rejoinder is often elicited by critiques of democracy. Would Winston Churchill have said about the adversary system what he said about democracy, that it is the worst form of government except all the others? Indeed, many an institution can be successfully defended by exhibiting the known alternatives, usually the historically superseded ones or those that hang on as anachronisms or those that serve the entrenched power of clearly visible elite groups. Still, I submit, the absence of known or tested preferred alternatives is hardly a definitive justification for any institution that exhibits glaring shortcomings. All progress begins with questioning the inevitability of the existing state of affairs.

Let us, for a moment, return to the liberal-democratic concept of law – what a Marxist would disapprovingly call the idealistic conception – that of a mechanism of social cohesion and intrasocietal conflict resolution. For law to function that way, the notions of justice on which law is assumed to be based should be *actually* internalized by society, not merely accepted formally. For instance, almost everyone will admit that if our North American legal system is to function the way it is supposed to, the facts actually pertaining to any case should be a crucial determinant of any verdict or adjudication. If a man is accused of a crime, then the truth of the matter – whether he actually did what is alleged or not – is of prime importance. On that basis, it is difficult to imagine any aspect of greater importance in the case, even though the circumstances of the act and the social consequences of various dispositions also merit consideration.

However, in the adversary system, whatever may be the devotion to truth on the part of the individuals who carry out the provisions of legal procedure, their actual efforts need not be directed toward the discovery and vindication of 'the actual facts.' On the contrary, if each side is to discharge its responsibility in the most effective manner, some effort must actually be directed toward the suppression of truth, as in taking advantage of rigidly established 'rules of evidence' in order to prevent facts or circumstances prejudicial to one's own side from coming to light.

It will be argued (and must be acknowledged) that rules of evidence and, in fact, the adversary system itself came into being in the process of creating a more equitable and humane system of justice. The presumption of innocence and the privilege accorded the accused to decline to testify are prominent examples. In the eyes of the law, a person accused is guilty of a crime if an impartial group of persons has been convinced that he is guilty, not necessarily if he is 'actually' guilty, and the rules of evidence are supposedly structured to put the onus of proof on the state rather than on the accused. Further, the prohibition against calling the accused to testify against himself is justified as a bulwark against torture, the usual manner of obtaining evidence where citizens have no protection against the all-powerful state and its agencies. In short, the adversary system, in institutionalizing a procedure whereby the state can be *challenged*, appears as a feature in the political evolution of curbs upon the absolute power of the state. The progressiveness of this development seems obvious to those who identify social progress with the diffusion of power, whereby, plainly speaking, the strong become weaker and the weak become stronger. However, in western liberal societies the state is not the only, perhaps not even the principal, centre of power. The nineteenth century saw a progressive concentration of power based on the control of economic resources, power wielded by groups not subjected to the sort of restrictions that democratic constitutions imposed on the state. Eventually, the excesses and abuses of that power led to political struggles, as a result of which some legal protection was extended to labour, to consumers, and to the public at large, in exemplary forms of guaranteeing the right to collective bargaining, of food and drug quality controls, regulation of public utilities, and so on. To the extent that such measures are enforced, they represent the 'social justice' function of the law – protection of the weak against the strong. The legal *procedures*, however, continue to function as before: in cases of alleged infringement of the law, they jealously guard the rights of the accused, when the accused is the strong against the weak.

Consider such crimes. The accused in this case is not the friendless wretch driven to crime by poverty, but may be a faceless corporation chiselling on the public, cutting corners on promises, conspiring to amass profits at the expense of the community or by pushing hapless competitors to the wall, evading taxes, polluting the environment, or what not – all crimes that only comparatively recently have become crimes in the light of attempts to curb ruthless abuses of economic power. For this type of criminal, the legal procedures designed to protect citizens against the all-powerful state become an arsenal of weapons in an on-going power struggle insensitive to citizen and community, certainly not 'safeguards against injustice.' Not only corporations but bona fide criminal syndicates employ permanent staffs of lawyers whose function is to facilitate the operations of their employers and to run interference against any attempts to inhibit these operations, regardless of whether they are or are not in 'the public interest.' It is impossible to avoid the conclusion that the role of the attorney in modern society is reduced to that of a henchman.

If the legal battle is reduced to one of resources, the function of law as the mobilization of right against might is subverted or exposed as an illusion, vindicating the Marxist thesis that in any society with a differentiated power structure the main purpose of the law is to protect the prerogatives of the strong (the dominant class).

Let us return to the question of alternatives. Pointedly, instances of criminals hiding behind the protective provisions of legal procedures are often cited and deplored. Invariably, arguments are advanced that these procedures are indispensable in all circumstances. Curb the right of the gangster to habeas corpus and you are helpless against the encroachments of a police state. Admit into court illegally obtained evidence that enables you to break up a vicious racket or a conspiracy to bleed the consumer, and you give the green light to unlimited invasions of citizens' privacy. I shall not pretend that these arguments can be refuted. They are convincing, and I know of no practical alternatives that can counteract the sterilization of the law as an instrument of justice while continuing to protect the citizen from abuses of state power. My purpose, however, is not to offer viable and practical alternatives but to call attention to the point that if law is conceived as an instrument of the resolution of intrasocietal conflicts a re-examination of the role of law in contemporary so-called democratic societies ought to focus on the predominant forms of conflict in those societies.

On occasion I have proposed a classification of all conflicts into three basic types.[4] This is not to suggest that any of these types is normally observed in its pure form, least of all in human affairs, but rather that human conflicts are usually mixtures of these components. The first type I call a *fight*. Here, each of the conflicting parties simply tries to eliminate the opponent from the scene of action, either by incapacitating him physically or by putting him to flight. The opponent is an enemy simply by virtue of being present. He is a noxious stimulus that elicits hostile reactions. Brawls, gang wars, clashes over possession of territory among animals and primitive human communities are examples of fights. It can be conceded that law in so-called civilized societies has served to reduce the incidence of fights.

The second type of conflict I call a *game*. Here the conflicting parties either by choice or by necessity must confine their aggressive acts to a specifically circumscribed range defined by the 'rules' of the game. The object of a game is not usually to eliminate or incapacitate the opponent as a living organism but to gain certain clearly specified objectives while adhering to the rules. Games of strategy, like chess or bridge, are the purest examples of game-like conflicts. The general meaning of 'game' is derived from these models. Wars as they were conducted by European states during the eighteenth and nineteenth centuries were, on the level of the chancelleries and of the high commands, more games than fights. On the level of battles fought and blood shed, the passions characteristic of the fight had plenty of outlets. But the planning and the strategic execution of those wars could be and was accomplished quite independently of hostile affect. In fact, the sovereigns and the generals – the principals of those conflicts – usually had considerable respect for each other, even admired each other's astuteness and competence, and so were not enemies except in a purely formal sense, in the same way that chess players, who may be close friends in 'real life,' are, formally speaking, 'enemies' over the chess board.

Conflicts generated by business competition are also primarily game-

4 See Rapoport, *Fights, Games and Debates* (1960).

like. The fact that business rivals seldom 'hate' each other does not prevent them from trying to ruin each others' position by elaborate stratagems and even taking pride in the results. Like sportsmen and military leaders, businessmen sometimes render grudging admiration to brilliant rival achievements of which they may have been the victims.

The third category of conflict I call a *debate*. The objective of a debate is neither to eliminate the opponent, as in a fight, nor to outwit him, as in a game, but to *convince* him, that is, induce him to see things in a different way. Clearly, a debate can be an instrument of conflict resolution only if the conflicting parties have some common ground of agreement. Partly, this common ground includes notions of what constitutes a reasonable procedure for ascertaining facts. In a conflict stemming from opposing views of what is 'true,' an agreed-upon method of ascertaining truth is clearly an aid to resolving the conflict. Conflicts also stem from differing views of what is just; again, some common ground of agreement concerning equity must exist in order for a debate to serve as an instrument of conflict resolution. In short, favourable conditions for resolving conflict by debate exist when the conflicting parties subscribe essentially to the same general ideas about the subject of dispute, when they see that the source of the conflict lies in the different emphases that each puts on one or another aspect of the matter. Thus, by bringing out all relevant facts and all relevant questions and weighing them against each other, a compromise solution is possible, one that does not award 'victory' to one side but is somehow most nearly in accord with the notions to which both sides subscribe.

Of these three idealized models of conflict, the game fits most closely the legal procedures of liberal-democratic societies. Formally, the clash of opposing sides in a court of law is supposed to be conducted in the manner of a debate. Actually, however, the principal feature of a genuine debate, as defined above, is absent. Certainly, the arguments made by each side are not designed to change the outlook of the other by way of convincing it of either the truth or the justice of the claims made. At best, the arguments are directed at third parties, specifically the judge or jury. More important, as has already been pointed out, neither the truth nor the justice of the matter at hand is, or need be, a primary consideration. The adversary system gives the strongest encouragement to stratagems, not to the clarification and searching analysis of the issues. People entrusted with the conduct of legal procedures are professionals; the professional's first responsibility is to the standards that define competence in the profession, and in law, as in most professions, these standards are largely very highly technical; competence is evaluated in terms of technical proficiency as demonstrated by successful outcomes of cases.

Ironically, professionalism is often thought of as a certification of integrity. A professional is supposed to be more concerned with the excellence of the service he provides than with any other aspects of his work (for instance, the remunerative ones). For the lawyer, this conception does not conflict with total loyalty to his client in the framework of the adversary system, for his role is so defined. It is quite different with other professionals called to testify as expert witnesses who are deliberately sought out for the particular opinions they hold. Such experts testifying for opposing sides are willy-nilly subjected to the pressures of the adversary system, even if their professional integrity is thereby endangered. Consider a psychiatrist called upon to testify to the sanity (or insanity) of a defendant: the legal procedure actually discourages his giving the most honest evaluation he is capable of. Honest evaluations of this condition are almost inevitably hedged by conjectures and reservations, never welcomed by the side on whose behalf the testimony is given. Worse, cross-examinations are often attempts to discredit the qualifications of an opposing witness – a grueling and humiliating experience that has driven many experts to vow never again to respond to such a demoralizing 'duty.' This is another way in which resources of knowledge, experience, and informed scientific opinion are not utilized in arriving at truth, as they might be if several experts were allowed to confer with each other or to confront each other in a genuine debate, all being concerned more with bringing out the truth of the matter than being made parties to stratagems and manœuvres. In fixating on the game aspects of conflict, the adversary system bars the way to the more sophisticated and productive concept of conflict as a debate – a confrontation between honestly held convictions.

This game-like conception of law as a competitive business is but one instance of the 'competicized' professionalism that pervades most functions in competitive societies. Similarly, professionalization of politics means that achievement of proficiency in political activity is the principal (often the sole) concern of the politician. (The first duty of the president, so the saying goes in the United States, is to get elected.) Success in politics amounts to the ability to forge coalitions that can capture and keep political power. What this power is used for is at best a secondary consideration, often altogether impertinent to the concerns of the politician. Professionalization of business management means developing techniques of survival in a competitive world. The viability – especially the expansion potential – of an enterprise becomes the primary goal of successful management. How, if at all, the 'health' of a business firm contributes to the health of the society as a whole or to the quality of life falls outside the scope of the genuine 'professional' manager's concern. Thereby, the 'ethics' of all professions tend to become only the 'rules of the game.' Predominance of the game concept of the workaday world is reflected in the language of the business community in America: occupations are referred to as games (e.g. the real estate game, the insurance game, the construction game). A bestselling book a few years ago was entitled *Games People Play*,[5] in which human relations are described as a network of intricate games. The game of 'Monopoly,' simulating business competition, has been replicated by many analogues, including one in which international politics is pictured as a struggle to conquer the world. The popularity enjoyed by such games indicates how accurately they portray the prevalent conception of what social life is all about.

Even more enlightening is the huge success of a certain type of crime fiction. In the United States most of the bestselling crime fiction depicts the private detective as a free enterpriser, outwitting powerful but less clever opponents. But in one series the hero is a lawyer. I am alluding to Perry Mason, whose superhuman powers reside in an uncanny ability to exploit the tricks of his trade. Necessarily, Mason is always on the side of justice; his efforts always result in clearing a suspect of a murder charge. However, since the outcome is known in advance (the plot is adhered to without exception), it is superfluous to the focus of real interest, which is the virtuosity of the hero who uses every conceivable form of deception and obfuscation in defending the interests of his client, yet keeps *formally* within the rules of the game, thus frustrating the attempts of his antagonists to neutralize him by disbarment or by criminal prosecution. As for his antagonists, the state attorney and his cohorts, they are simply out to 'get' Mason's client. There is no trace of evidence that these representatives of the law are interested in either truth or justice. Their minds are made up from the start by their own 'interests,' which are to find a scapegoat and obtain a conviction. I know of no stronger indictment of the adversary system than these stories. The indictment is not in the stories themselves (all highly stylized idealizations) but in their tremendous popularity, which reflects a profound internalization of the concept of justice identified with the triumph of cleverness.

In summary, the professionalization of legal procedures and the inter-

---

5 Berne *Games People Play: the Psychology of Human Relationships* (1964)

nalization of competition as the primary mode of social life reinforce each other. Both deflect attention from the concept of law as an instrument of justice and equitable conflict resolution, supposedly a tenet of faith in liberal-democratic societies.

Another influence that has contributed to the conceptual separation of law and justice derives from the Anglo-Saxon philosophical tradition, known in its various manifestations as empiricism, positivism, pragmatism, instrumentalism, and operationalism. In this tradition, represented by its foremost exponents, Francis Bacon, John Locke, David Hume, and John Stuart Mill, concrete experience and the evidence of the senses are viewed as the only sources of true knowledge. It is this orientation that has nurtured the growth of experimental science and has linked scientific knowledge with the practical achievements of modern technology. In America it gave rise to pragmatism, the conception of truth as 'that which works,' and brought to the forefront of public admiration the 'practical man,' rich in know-how and contemptuous of 'theory' and 'speculation.'

The pragmatic attitude was most succinctly expressed by the foremost American jurist, Oliver Wendell Holmes, in his famous dictum: 'Prophecies of what courts will do in fact and nothing more pretentious are what I mean by the law.'[6] Holmes' record reveals no evidence that he himself as a thinker and a man of good will was indifferent to law as an instrument of justice. On the contrary. Holmes was an ardent guardian of the rights of the individual against encroachment by forces more powerful than he, quite in the spirit of the idealistic intents of the United States constitution. A different interpretation of his dictum suggests itself, namely, that abstract conceptions of justice transcending the practices of his own society are of no concern to the jurist. Indeed, the method of legal education introduced by the Harvard Law School (the so-called case study method), being inspired by positivist philosophy, was designed to emphasize familiarity with the concrete realities of legal procedures rather than concern with general and abstract principles of justice. The pragmatic definition of professional competence is in terms of knowledge of relevant techniques.

It is interesting to see the form taken by this pragmatic approach to laws when applied to a conception of international law. Here, Holmes' dictum might well be modified to read 'Prophecies of what the *litigants* will do and nothing more pretentious is what we mean by international law.' At least

6 Holmes *Collected Legal Papers* (1920), at 173

this is the impression one gets from an article on international law by Edward McWhinney, for which Holmes' dictum appropriately serves as the motto. Reviewing the confrontations between the United States and the Soviet Union throughout the cold war, McWhinney sounds a cautious note of optimism:

> In truth, though traditional international law has often been more notable for its breach than its observance in recent years, these Cold War 'minimum rules of the game' have been with us for quite some time now. And in so far as they may reflect, far more nearly than traditional international law doctrine in the areas of Cold War conflict, the working facts of present-day East-West international relations with their actual record of accommodations and adjustments of conflicting interests of the rival power blocs, they may ... meet the ultimate pragmatist test of the usefulness of any theory, whether of international law or otherwise, that they seem to work.[7]

The pragmatic or positivist conceptions of law, characteristic of Anglo-Saxon tradition, and their counterparts in conceptions of international relations, the so-called 'realist' view, have the advantage of being closely related to what is actually observed. If a theory is valued for its descriptive accuracy, certainly what is actually observed must serve as a point of departure. Then long departures by way of extrapolations and abstractions from observable data tend to be viewed with suspicion. In the positivist conception, law is the totality of legal *procedures*, nothing else. So, in this conception, the key to a theory of international relations is the way they are actually conducted, which means that such a theory must be rooted in the relative power positions of sovereign states responsible to no one and constrained by nothing except the realities of power.

One can, however, ask more of a theory than merely an accurate description of the existing state of affairs, especially of a theory dealing with institutions that affect human relations. For, although it is possible to view institutions as evolving by force of circumstance, it is also permissible – in fact, sometimes imperative – to view institutions through the prisms of values. A theory that takes values into account is called a normative theory. Its task is not only to describe how things are but also how they might be and to compare the actual with the potential or the intended, to note the discrepancies, to analyze their genesis and, if possible, indicate ways of bringing the actual into greater accord with the desired. It is on this

---

7 2 Falk and Mendlovitz eds, *The Strategy of World Order* (1966), at 228

score that the pragmatic and the so-called 'realist' theories fail. They are based on a philosophy that seeks to separate the cognitive from the evaluative aspect of cognition. Pragmatists and 'realists' are deeply suspicious of what they call 'visionary' outlooks. The suspicion is not unfounded, because visionary outlooks often blind us to what we have to cope with. On the other hand, without visions of some sort that go beyond the immediately perceivable and usable within the existing framework of values, man would be forever condemned to the consequences of his past short-sightedness; for the most 'practical' solutions of yesterday's problems are frequently the most oppressive deadweight barring the way to the solutions of the ominously pressing problems of today.

ANATOL RAPOPORT, a graduate of the University of Chicago, is a professor of psychology and mathematics at the University of Toronto, having come from the University of Michigan in 1970. He is well known for his work on game theory and is the editor of the Game Theory Section of the *Journal of Conflict Resolution*. He is the author of ten books, including *Fights, Games and Debates* (1960) and *Prisoners' Dilemma* (1965).

ANTHONY DOOB

Psychology and evidence

Whenever I, as a psychologist, look at the history of my field's contribution to law, I am struck by the fact that we seem to ignore what we do best and emphasize what we do worst. Psychology, in its present state of development, seems to be fairly good at answering questions such as, Is the presence of A more likely to lead to result C than the presence of B? or If a witness says X, is that likely to increase, decrease, or not affect the probability of his being believed as compared to the situation in which he does not say X? For the most part, questions put in this way are questions that can be tested empirically, and tentative conclusions to these questions can be drawn.

Unfortunately, this is not the kind of question that psychologists are usually asked to answer. Instead, if one were to record systematically the questions asked of psychologists, one would find that they are much more likely to be of the kind X is an A; Y is a B; Who did C? or If my witness says X, will he be believed? Generally speaking, I think that psychologists, like the rest of mankind, are not good at answering these questions when they relate to complex social behaviour. More to the point, it is extremely rare for the psychologist to have any special knowledge or training that allows him to answer these kinds of questions any more accurately than anyone else. This leaves us, then, with the question of what psychologists actually can contribute to law, given the premise that they are not generally very good at predicting individual complex behaviour.

Wigmore[1] noted the same problem in the second edition of his *Principles*

---

1 Wigmore *Principles of Judicial Proof*, (2d ed, 1931), at 530–1

of Judicial Proof, observing that, since any generalizations to come from psychologists would be true only 'in general' and not for a specific case, the generalizations were, for the most part, of little use to the legal profession. As Greer[2] has pointed out, however, 'Wigmore's criticism that psychologists' findings do not apply to the individual witness seems to overlook an important point. Many, if not most, rules of evidence are in fact actuarial, i.e. based on probability. Thus a particular witness is precluded from giving hearsay evidence, not after an examination to test whether his evidence is true or false, but because hearsay evidence is considered to be *in general* unreliable.'

This, then, gives the psychologist one important area of work in which his research might be useful – testing some of the general legal propositions that are in fact assumptions about the way in which human beings process information.

Nevertheless, as Meehl[3] has pointed out, 'Psychologists should be cautious when an alleged principle of modern behavioural science appears to conflict [with what lawyers believe to be the case].' The lesson, I think, is that we have to be very sceptical of any kind of generalization. This is, however, no more true in the area of psychology and law than in any other area where the findings of the behavioural sciences are being applied.

An example of the kind of research that deals with general questions in the law comes from some research at the University of Toronto into the effects on an accused person of section 12 of the Canada Evidence Act.[4] This section has the effect of allowing information concerning previous criminal convictions of an accused person to be presented as evidence of his credibility but not directly of his guilt or innocence. Under this section of the Act, the trier of fact is allowed to use the information about previous convictions for one purpose (determining credibility) but not for another purpose (determining guilt or innocence). In correlational research, others have shown that people who have had previous criminal convictions (or who do not take the witness stand on their own behalf) are more likely to be convicted than people who have had no previous convictions.[5] Unfortunately, this research does not provide answers to two important questions: 1/ Could these findings be explained by the fact that the cases against those with previous convictions might have been stronger than the cases against

2 Greer, 'Anything but the truth? The reliability of testimony in criminal trials,' (1971), 11 *Brit. J. Crim.*, 131 at 141–2
3 Meehl, 'Law and the Fireside Inductions: Some Reflections of a Clinical Psychologist,' (1971), 27 *J. Soc. Iss.*, 65 at 85
4 R.S.C. 1970, C.E–10
5 Kalven and Zeisel *The American Jury* (1966), at 159–62

those without convictions? and 2/ Can limiting instructions from the trial judge work to restrict the use of information as they are designed to do?

In addition, there is, of course, the question whether previous convictions of a witness make it more likely that he will not tell the truth on the witness stand. In other words, does the fact of one or more criminal convictions make it more likely that the person will lie? The nature of our language would lead us to believe that a convicted criminal would be more likely to give false evidence in a trial. Thus, we refer to people who have been convicted of almost any criminal offense as 'dishonest.' This leads to the inference that if a person is dishonest in one way (e.g. he is a thief) he will be dishonest in another way (e.g. give false evidence at his own trial). Interestingly enough, psychological research does not support this kind of inference. The more general question, obviously, concerns the generality of 'moral behaviour.' After reviewing the evidence in this area the psychologist Walter Mischel concluded that 'the data on moral behaviour provide no support for the widespread psychodynamic belief in ... a unitary trait entity of conscience or honesty.'[6] From the existing data, therefore, we cannot justify the inference that a person who has been dishonest in one situation will be dishonest in another. More specifically, the data would suggest that just because a person has been found guilty at one time in his life of a criminal offence, one should not conclude that he is more likely to give false or misleading evidence than a person who had never been convicted. Obviously, however, if a person had been shown to be someone who had given false evidence in a similar situation some time in the past, the assumption that he would give false evidence at the time in question might be more justified.

Quite independently of the psychological reality of the situation, then, the trier of fact is being asked to use the evidence of previous criminal convictions to make inferences about the credibility of the witness, but he is asked specifically to disregard this evidence in his inferences about the guilt or innocence of the accused. As Friedland has pointed out, 'to say that the accused is a bad man and is not to be believed is hardly distinguishable from saying that he is a bad man and is guilty of the offence. Moreover, to tell the jury, as must now be done, that the evidence is not admissible to show disposition may only increase the likelihood that it will be so used. Indeed, knowing the accused's record, the jury may give the evidence even greater weight than it properly deserves on the question of disposition.'[7]

6 Mischel *Personality and Assessment* (1968), at 26
7 Friedland, 'Comment,' (1969), 47 *Can. Bar Rev.*, 656 at 658

The critical question, therefore, becomes whether the instructions can work. Once again, this assumption seems to have very little support in the psychological literature. The assumption that people can take evaluative information and differentiate its use efficiently according to external instructions goes directly against the research done on the 'halo effect.' This well-documented phenomenon is simply people's tendency to infer positive characteristics about a person when they hear a few positive things about him and to infer negative characteristics about a person when they hear negative things about him.[8]

With respect to section 12 of the Canada Evidence Act, it would thus follow that if a trier of fact were to hear that an accused person had a criminal record, he would be likely to think of this accused as a generally bad person. When he is then asked to judge whether or not the accused is guilty of the offence for which he is being tried, he would be likely to infer that the accused was guilty. The problem is that even if he is told to disregard the evidence of previous criminal convictions when deciding guilt the damage has been done. The trier of fact may feel that he is not using the evidence improperly, but if he thinks of the accused as being generally bad, he is likely to infer that he is guilty.

A second, more insidious, way in which the evidence of previous misconduct can hurt the accused is the possible relaxing of the standard of proof necessary for a finding of guilt. Thus a trier of fact may feel that it would not be so bad to find a 'criminal' guilty when he did not do the crime in question as it would be to find a person guilty who, in fact, was innocent and had never been convicted before.[9]

Interestingly enough, there are some situations when the courts clearly feel that limiting instructions could not possibly have the effect for which they are intended. In *The Queen* v *Times Square Cinema*, for example, Chief Justice Gale of the Ontario Court of Appeal, in coming to the conclusion that certain survey results were quite properly kept from the jury, states that 'to present them at all would likely so mislead the jury as to render impotent any warning by the Judge that they should be ignored.'[10] I do not know how far he would be willing to extend his assumption that people are not always able to limit the use to which they put evidence, but

---

8 See, for example, Rosenberg and Olshan, 'Evaluative and descriptive aspects in personality perception,' (1970), 16 *J. Pers. and Soc. Psych.*, 619.

9 For a discussion of this and related phenomena, see Lerner 'The desire for justice and reactions to victims,' in Macaulay and Berkowitz eds, *Altruism and Helping Behaviour* (1970), at 205–29.

10 *Regina* v *Times Square Cinema Ltd*, (1971), 4 C.C.C. (2d), 229 at 233

clearly he is of the opinion that in at least some situations it does not work.

One advantage that a psychologist has in looking at a problem such as this one is that he can sometimes determine ways to test the various assumptions experimentally. This is what Hershi Kirshenbaum and I did in the experiment mentioned earlier.[11] The experiment was designed to discover the effects of the provisions of section 12 of the Canada Evidence Act on the likelihood of conviction of an accused person. More specifically, we wanted to find out whether a man with previous convictions was more likely to be seen as guilty of an offence with which he was charged than a man without previous convictions. At the same time we wished to find out whether there was any possibility that instructions to limit the use of such information could be effective.

The method was quite straightforward. A group of forty-eight people were divided into two main experimental conditions. In the 'control' conditions, the subjects were asked to read a short summary of a hypothetical case of a man charged with breaking and entering; about four hundred words long, it asked the reader to 'imagine that you are a juror listening to a case of a man accused of breaking and entering. After you have read this you will be asked to indicate whether you would recommend that the accused person be found guilty or innocent of the charge.' These subjects received no information about previous criminal behaviour of the accused. Presumably they assumed that there was no criminal record, but this was not explicitly stated.

Another group of subjects were told in addition that 'the accused man took the stand but did not give any important evidence. However, while on the witness stand, it was established that he had been convicted five different times of breaking and entering private homes and had also been convicted twice of being in possession of stolen property.'

Finally, a group of subjects received all this information but in addition were told that 'in his instructions to the jury, the judge pointed out that by law the accused person's previous criminal record should only be used to determine whether or not he is to be believed as a witness and that it should not be used to determine whether or not he is guilty.' Obviously, what we were interested in were the subjects' answers to a question that was put to them after they have finished reading: 'How likely do you think it is that he is guilty?'

The results were very simple. Subjects who had received information

11 For a more complete description of this research, see Doob and Kirshenbaum, 'Some Empirical Evidence on the Effect of s. 12 of the Canada Evidence Act upon an Accused,' (1972), 15 *Crim.L.Q.* 88.

about the previous convictions of the accused were much more likely to think him guilty than subjects who had not. Most important, however, was the fact that the instructions about the limited use to which the convictions could be put had no effect.

A number of things should be said about this experiment. In the first place, it was a heterogeneous sample of people who volunteered for the experiment. They were recruited and interviewed in the Ontario Science Centre, in city parks, outside supermarkets, and in various public buildings. Secondly, the experiment was loaded in favour of the judge's limiting instructions. They were the last thing read by the subject before he was asked to indicate his judgment of guilt, and yet they had no effect on the decision. Thus the demands on the subject were very strong to think 'Yes, what they are trying to do is to tell me that I shouldn't use the information about the previous convictions in coming to my decision, and I'll try to be good and follow the instructions that they have given me.' I suspect that this kind of thing happens when a jury hears about previous criminal behaviour of an accused and is then told that they should not use it in determining the guilt or innocence of the accused. They probably try not to use the information – then they walk into the jury room thinking that he is guilty (or at least more likely to be guilty than if he did not have a criminal record). Alternatively, the jury member may shift his criterion of the standard of proof necessary to determine guilt and feel that it would not be so bad to find an innocent accused guilty if he had a criminal record.

I would suspect, however, that in most cases the members of a jury *try* to follow the judge's instructions as best they can. Thus most members of the jury would probably not talk about the accused's previous convictions nor use this information in arguing their position to other members of the jury. Unfortunately, section 576.2 of the Criminal Code, by forbidding members of the jury to reveal anything of their deliberations, makes it impossible for researchers in Canada to get this kind of information directly.

Wigmore criticized the use of psychological evidence on the ground that a large number of instances would be needed to draw any kind of safe generalization. Obviously this is a valid statement, but if simulations are acceptable, a large number of instances can, in fact, be achieved. Another relevant criticism by Wigmore is that the situation involved in a 'simulation' is very different from that in a real court room in two important ways: the motives of partisan litigation are not present, and the situation is not emotionally charged because in the experiment important consequences do not follow the participant's decision. Although both of these factors are clearly absent from the simulations used in this and other similar experiments, the effect of their absence must be considered. I would not deny that subjects are probably less concerned about the 'verdict' in a simulation; similarly, they clearly spend less time considering possible outcomes in a simulation than they would in a 'real' case. However, would variables such as these affect the over-all relationships found in this experiment? I think not. In the same vein, I do not feel it to be critical that the sample of subjects used in this experiment was not exactly comparable to that used in actual jury trials. It is a case, once again, of there being a difference between the method used here and the situation to which we would like to generalize the results. But it is hard to imagine how this rather heterogeneous sample would produce a pattern of results markedly different from those derived from a sample drawn from a different population.

As far as I can see, the major value of experiments such as these is to point out the kinds of factors that affect the judgments made in a trial. The results of the experiment in no way 'prove' that previous criminal convictions should be excluded from consideration in a criminal trial. Presumably, a number of other considerations should be weighed before such a decision can be made. However, the results do suggest that the particular way in which this evidence is now admissible in our courts is probably inappropriate – the evidence is admitted for one purpose but is used by well-meaning people for another.

These conclusions are consistent with the results of similar experiments recently published by the London School of Economics Jury Project in England.[12] Experimenters found that previous similar convictions increased the likelihood of a guilty verdict. However, their 'judicial instructions' were to disregard the evidence completely. In cases of theft the juries receiving such instructions tended to find more guilty verdicts than did control juries who received no information about previous convictions, but the instructions did have some effect in reducing convictions. Because of this important difference in the nature of the judicial instructions, direct comparisons cannot be made. In any case, however, it is clear that previous similar criminal convictions do increase the likelihood of a finding of guilt.[13]

This research is most clearly applicable for those interested in looking at our present rules of evidence with the thought of changing them. It is not as relevant to the individual practising lawyer who wants some help in arguing

12 Cornish and Sealy, 'Juries and the Rules of Evidence,' (1973), *Crim. L.Rev.* 208
13 The LSE project also had some juries that deliberated on a case of rape. However, because the method of introducing the evidence of previous convictions was markedly different from that used here the results are not discussed.

specific aspects of his case or to the court in deciding for one party or the other, and it is in matters like these that psychologists tend to get involved – areas in which they have not yet shown their competence. But I think that between these two extremes the psychologist can make contributions that may have relevance to the specific issues in question in a trial.

To illustrate this, I will draw on some data that Kirshenbaum and I collected related to a specific case that came up for trial (twice) in Toronto.[14] The case involved a rather standard robbery of a large department store. As far as I can see, the only substantial question in the trial was the identity of the men who staged the robbery and the manner in which these identifications were made. It was a complicated case, involving a number of different men, and most of the details are not really relevant, but the important point was that one of the defendants, Ronald Shatford, had been picked out of a police lineup by one of the witnesses – the cashier who had been robbed. As Glanville Williams has pointed out, 'all that an identification parade can really be said to establish is that the accused resembled the criminal more closely than any other members of the parade did, which is not saying very much.'[15] Much has been written on the problems of identification,[16] and all that need be said about it here is that it is a very difficult problem.

A psychologist, it seemed to me, should be able to look at a situation like this and develop some plausible hypotheses to explain why it is that a witness to a crime might be able to pick someone he had never seen before out of a lineup. One obvious reason for such an incorrect identification might be that the accused person closely resembled the actual offender. But there are enough cases where this is not so[17] to suggest that other factors must be operative.

A number of aspects must be considered. In the first place, it seems reasonable to assume that most witnesses are going to try to do a good job for the police and will even try very hard to help the police convict the person who committed the crime. Most witnesses, when presented with someone whom the police are convinced committed the crime, are likely to err in the direction of agreeing with the police rather than disagreeing. Williams also points out that 'identification seems to be a matter on which personal pride has a strong effect: a witness often resents it when his ability

14 For a more complete description of this research, see Doob and Kirshenbaum, 'Bias in Police Lineups – Partial Remembering,' (1973), 1 *J. of Pol. Sci. and Admin.*, 287.
15 Williams *The Proof of Guilt* (3d ed, 1963), at 121
16 See, for example, Wall *Eyewitness Identification in Criminal Cases* (1965), at 46.
17 Ibid, 23

to recognize someone is questioned.'[18] Among other things, Williams is suggesting that witnesses are likely to become easily committed to what they have said in identifying a suspect, and as a result are unlikely to change their opinion about whether or not a suspect was the person whom they saw committing a crime.

Assuming that a witness is going to try to do a good job for the police, we can expect that the witness who does not have a very good memory of the event in question will undoubtedly use whatever information he has to help in the identification. If this partial information fits the police suspect, it is likely that the suspect will be identified as the offender even though in other ways he may not resemble the actual offender at all. For example, if a witness had given the police a description of the offender consisting of such rather vague characteristics as 'he had strange eyes' or 'he was rather attractive,' then this witness would be likely to pick someone out of a police lineup who fits this rather vague description. In the case of the identification of Ronald Shatford, this is precisely what Kirshenbaum and I suggest had happened. Shatford was accused of robbing a department store of about $7000. The cashier who was robbed could not give the police a very good description of the offender; she admitted to being very afraid and remembered only that the men who robbed her were 'very neatly dressed, and rather good looking, and they looked enough alike to be brothers.'[19] But she was able to pick Shatford out of a lineup consisting of Shatford and eleven other 'distractors.'

It was this actual identification that Kirshenbaum and I set out to try to explain. The only piece of information to go on was the cashier's earlier description of the offender as 'rather attractive.' The other two pieces of information were obviously of little use in explaining the identification of one person from the group of twelve. The obvious hypothesis that occurred to us was that Shatford was picked out of the lineup precisely because he was the most attractive in the group of twelve. This, obviously, is a question amenable to empirical verification. If Shatford was indeed the most attractive of the twelve men, then this would support the hypothesis that part of the reason he was chosen was that the key witness remembered only a little bit about the offender and used this information to pick one man out of the twelve who participated in the lineup.

Luckily, in this case, a picture of the police lineup was available to us. Twenty female subjects were then asked to rate each of the people (on an

18 Williams, supra note 15, at 113
19 Haggart, 'The bizarre story of two brothers and a holdup,' (3 July 1971) *Toronto Telegram* at 1

eleven-point scale ranging from 'extremely good looking' to 'definitely not good looking'). Of the twelve men in the lineup, the police suspect was rated significantly more attractive than any of the other men in the lineup. In fact, of the 220 comparisons between the suspect and each of the distractors for each of the twenty subjects, the suspect was rated as the more attractive 179 times, the suspect and one of the distractors were rated equally attractive twenty-three times, and one of the distractors was rated more attractive eighteen times. One cannot question the notion that the accused was seen as the most attractive in the group.

It is conceivable, however, that when actually picking a suspect, people would, for inexplicable reasons, choose someone else. In order to test this, twenty-one other female subjects were shown the same picture and asked to 'imagine you were a witness to a crime. All you can remember about the criminal is that he was rather good looking. The police then arrest someone whom they think committed the crime, and they place him in a lineup. Imagine that you are shown this lineup, and asked by the police to identify the guilty person. The police seem certain that they have the right person, but they need your identification. You try your best to pick out the guilty man. In the picture below, whom would you pick?' If choices like this were completely random, we would expect the accused to be chosen about one-twelfth of the time (or about twice by the twenty-one subjects). In fact, he was chosen eleven times, considerably more than chance.

In one sense all that we have done in these studies is to show that factors not amenable to physical measurement can bias an identification. The problem, of course, is that such things as height, race, weight, etc are subject to easy, almost perfectly reliable, measurement. Something vague like 'attractiveness' is harder to measure, but in this case, at least, the data are extremely consistent. It is interesting to note that the police in a situation such as this one would probably not have considered putting the suspect in a lineup with people who were markedly different from him on such dimensions as height, race, etc, especially if these were the charac-teristics remembered by the witness, but as soon as the variable is a bit more vague it is apparently not considered by the police in constructing a lineup.

All these data do is provide a plausible explanation for the identification. One explanation is that the suspect actually did commit the crime and the witness is absolutely correct in her identification. An alternative explana-tion is that anybody operating on this minimal information could have done the same, even though such a person might never have had any contact with the accused man. This alternative explanation should act to weaken the case against the accused. It is important to note that a psychologist cannot say anything directly about whether or not the man accused of the crime actually did it. All that a psychologist can honestly do in a situation like this is to comment on (and do research on) the value of certain aspects of the evidence in the case.

Rather interesting problems arise when one considers the admissibility of data such as this in a criminal trial. Not being a lawyer, I will not go into great detail about this question, but since these data would appear at first glance to be very similar to 'survey' evidence, it is perhaps worthwhile to compare the two approaches. The most basic question is whether these are survey data and, if so, whether the standards for the admissibility of these data would be the same as those for the admissibility of other survey data. I will use for comparison the Manitoba Court of Appeal case of *Regina* v *Prairie Schooner News*[20] and the Ontario Court of Appeal case of *Regina* v *Times Square Cinema*.[21]

One critical matter, as was pointed out in the opinion of Freedman JA in *Prairie Schooner News* is that the sample be representative of the population to which you wish to generalize, and what this means in practice depends on the nature and purpose of the survey. Thus, unless one were to argue in the case of the *Prairie Schooner News* that forty-three students in a sociology course and twenty-five employees of the CNR were representative of 'all Canadians' one would have to say that the survey was a bad one. Similarly, the survey run in the *Times Square Cinema* case had a strongly biased sample: A/ those who would respond to an advertisement to see a dirty movie free and B/ those who responded to a telephone call to go see a dirty movie. In the case of the *Times Square Cinema*, therefore, I think I would agree with Gale CJO that these surveys 'are to me so unsatisfactory and inconclusive of a fair test of community standards of acceptance as to have no probative value whatever.'[22] However, had the designers of the surveys been a little more sensible in choosing their sample, the court might have been more sympathetic in considering the survey evidence.

These surveys (and most other surveys bearing on obscenity cases) have one important aspect in common that differentiates them from the studies on identification just described – the surveys in *Prairie Schooner News* and *Times Square Cinema* were designed to get an accurate estimate of the opinion of 'Canadians in general.' In the studies of the lineup, the

20 (1970) 1 C.C.C. (2d), at 251
21 (1971) 4 C.C.C. (2d), at 229
22 Ibid, at 232

question being asked was quite different – whether a group of people would rate the accused man as more attractive than the distractors.

More to the point, it is impossible for me to construct a hypothesis to explain how the sample of subjects used in our identification studies created the effects we got. On the other hand, it is rather easy to see how the samples of people used in the obscenity cases could have come up with results that did not fit what most Canadians feel.

In conclusion: I have tried to demonstrate two kinds of contributions psychologists can make to the legal process – one in the area of testing the effects of various rules of evidence and procedure and the other in the general area of testing specific propositions in specific cases. In neither case, however, do I feel that the court should turn to the psychologist to act as the trier of fact. The psychologist is no more skilled at this than is anyone else. All the psychologist can do is aid the court in giving the proper weight to certain kinds of evidence.

ANTHONY DOOB received an A B from Harvard and a PH D from Stanford and is an associate professor in the Department of Psychology, University of Toronto. He has just completed a term as associate chairman of the department and is a consultant to the Law Reform Commission of Canada on the law of evidence. He is at present engaged in a study at the Centre of Criminology of discretion in the juvenile justice system.

CHARLES HANLY

Psychopathology of the trial process

INTRODUCTION

Any human process is vulnerable to the hazards of psychopathological disturbance, that is, a disturbance which distorts or inhibits some mental activity or behaviour. Individual development and family relationships have received most attention thus far by psychoanalysts, and for an obvious reason – they are the ultimate determinants of psychopathology wherever else it may be found in human relationships and hence have been the focus of both scientific investigation and therapeutic intervention. But as the Greek poets and philosophers already preconsciously knew, psychopathology can make its influence felt in any area – the rise and fall of gods and kings, the choice of political leaders, or the preference for various forms of social and political order. In any case, it is reasonable to assume that the venerability and sanctity of the law do not immunize jurors, lawyers, and judges against the influence of unconscious processes while in court. The trial process is therefore vulnerable to psychopathological disturbance, with the result that justice may not be done or it may be done as the result of chance rather than by rational design. Any study of psychopathological aspects of the trial process has as many points of departure as there are principals in the courtroom action. This paper concerns the jury.[1]

---

1 There is a considerable literature applying psychoanalysis to the study of criminality, legal punishment, the sentencing of criminals, the prevention of crime, and the nature of law, liability, and contracts. See Freud, 'The Expert Opinion in the Halsmann Case,' (1961), 21 *Standard Edition of the Complete Psychological Works of Sigmund Freud (S.E.),* at

METHOD

It is important at the outset to be clear about the limits inherent in the approach being taken by this study. The theoretical argument rests on five psychoanalytic principles. They will be used as the basis for raising certain issues concerning trial procedures and typical events as they may affect the processes of thought, observation, memory, and feeling aroused in jurors during a trial and can be expected to influence their decision significantly. The unconscious aspects of these processes can be inferred only on the basis of independently established psychoanalytic theories, given the constraints imposed on the collection of relevant data. Consequently, anything said about them is probable only. Probable statements can be useful, however, in identifying and illuminating certain psychological issues inherent in the trial process.

In order to gain a somewhat greater degree of probability and provide references to an actual trial these psychoanalytic considerations have been linked to a particular trial – that of Stephen Truscott at Goderich, Ontario, in 1959.

In June 1959 a twelve-year-old girl, Lynne Harper, was raped and strangled. Her body was found in a woodlot near the RCAF station at Clinton, Ontario. She was the daughter of an officer at the station. The family lived in the married quarters on the base. Stephen Truscott, then a fourteen-year-old boy, the son of a warrant officer whose family also lived in the married quarters, was charged with the girl's murder and, subsequently, in September of the same year, found guilty of the crime by a jury at Goderich in Huron County, the county where the crime was committed. He was sentenced to be hanged. An appeal to the Court of Appeal for Ontario was dismissed,[2] but on the same day his sentence was commuted

251–3, and 'Psycho-Analysis and the Establishment of the Facts in Legal Proceedings,' (1959), 9 *S.E.* 103–14; Balint, 'On Punishing Offenders,' in Wilbur and Muensterberger *Psycho-analysis and Culture* (1951) 254–79; Desmonde, 'Psycho-analysis and Legal Origins,' (1953), 34 *Internl. J. Psycho-an.* 52; Ehrenzweig, 'Civil Liability,' (1953), 10 *Amer. Imago* 15; Bienenfeld, 'Justice, Aggression and Eros,' (1957), 38 *Internl. J. Psycho-an.* 419; Abrahamsen *The Psychology of Crime* (1960); Ehrenzweig *Psychoanalytic Jurisprudence* (1971). Two works, influenced by psychoanalysis have been contributed by Frank, *Law and the Modern Mind* (1930) and *Courts on Trial* (1969). However, there is very little in the literature concerning psychological factors at work in the trial process itself or more particularly in the jury. A recent work is Schoenfeld *Psychoanalysis and the Law* (1973); see also Reiwald *Society and its Criminals* (1949). The University of Chicago sponsored a study of jury deliberative processes but the researchers were obliged to abandon it.

2 (1960) 126 C.C.C. 109

to life imprisonment by the federal government. An application for leave to appeal to the Supreme Court of Canada was refused. But as a result of public concern aroused by a book written by Isabel LeBourdais, *The Trial of Stephen Truscott*,[3] the federal cabinet in 1966 asked the Supreme Court of Canada to review the trial and any further evidence it might wish to consider. The Supreme Court upheld the findings of the trial court, with one judge, Mr Justice Hall,[4] dissenting. Stephen Truscott was released from prison on parole in 1969.

For this study, parts of the trial transcript and the appeal books used in the Supreme Court of Canada were examined and some of the jurors interviewed. These interviews had a number of unavoidable limitations. They relied on the memory of the jurors, refreshed occasionally by rereading of material from the transcript during the interviews; thus, they were subject to the usual technical problems associated with remembering emotionally significant events some thirteen years before. And they posed two additional problems. The trial and the original sentence had caused a public sensation, horrifying liberal public opinion and prompting criticism of the trial. Subsequently, the book by LeBourdais had been critical of the jury. These post-trial experiences made jurors feel defensive and under an obligation to justify their actions as though in expectation of criticisms. For this reason only four of the seven jurors now alive and well agreed to be interviewed.

It is not the intention of this paper to make generalizations about the Truscott jury per se, but rather to use the trial as a means of illustrating the kinds of difficulties any juror can be expected to encounter in carrying out the exacting obligation placed upon him by the law under the circumstances of a criminal trial.

A more significant difficulty for enquiries of this kind in the long run is the law, introduced in 1972, which makes it an offence for a juror to make any statement concerning anything that transpired when the jury was absent from the courtroom.[5] As a result, a proper psychoanalytic study of the actual processes by which jurors reach decisions is prevented. Such a study would require that jurors be able to associate freely and communicate all of their associations without inhibition, inevitably including memories of what had occurred in the jury room. The situation parallels a

---

3 LeBourdais *The Trial of Stephen Truscott* (1966)

4 [1967] S.C.R. 309

5 s. 576.2 of the Criminal Code. A helpful discussion of the legal issues involved in the prohibition against jurors disclosing what took place in the jury room is found in Williams *The Proof of Guilt* (3d ed, 1963) 266–71. In reference to the situation in Britain, where no

revealing incident from Freud's psychoanalytic practice. Freud was once approached by a senior official of the Austrian government wishing to be psychoanalysed. During the interview he informed Freud that it had to be understood that he could not communicate anything bearing upon secrets of state. Freud refused to analyse him, not because he wanted to know the secrets of the Austrian state, but because this inhibition on communication would inevitably be used by the patient as an ironclad resistance to communicating secrets of his personal life without which the analysis could not work. But, of course, our purposes are different. We are only trying to gain some insight into the ways in which psychopathology may interfere with the rational pursuit of justice in trials. Nevertheless, these limitations mean that any possible insight is limited to reasonable conjecture and cannot ever acquire the status of scientific truth. Some, no doubt, will want to reject the undertaking as having no validity at all for this reason, but that would be a mistake.

There is also a problem of definition. What constitutes psychopathology in the context of a trial? In general, psychopathology refers to mental processes in individuals which make it impossible for them to deal adequately with reality. The question which then arises is how one defines reality in this context. It is assumed here that reality is defined by the law governing the conduct of trials, the rules of evidence in particular, and the evidence presented to the court. These are the realities with which jurors have to cope in carrying out their responsibility. Thus, for example, the law requires that the jurors deem the accused person to be innocent until his guilt has been established beyond a reasonable doubt. The failure to function in this way on the part of a juror would then constitute evidence of a psychopathological disturbance, for he would have failed to act according to the objective demands of the situation. Or, again, the law requires that jurors base their finding on the evidence presented to the court and on nothing else. In so far as the jury finds on the basis of the evidence as presented, even though the evidence may turn out to have been incomplete or badly presented, there can be no question of psychopathology. The jury

similar law forbidding disclosure exists, Williams offers the following: 'It is at least to be hoped that, if any action is taken to forbid disclosure of the jury's deliberations, exemption will be given for disclosure made on public grounds, or for the purpose of genuine enquiry into the jury system' (270). Surely these grounds for exemption should be recognized in Ontario's legislation. So long as the prohibition against disclosure is maintained, the observations needed to make an objective study of the actual working of the jury during the crucial stage of its deliberations will remain concealed. The legislation is antiscientific in effect.

would have dealt adequately with reality as defined by the legal context within which they must function. On the other hand, in so far as a juror systematically overlooks or denies certain important evidence, or arbitrarily denies it in favour of other evidence, we can reasonably suppose that his observing and thinking has been subject to the influence of a psychological disturbance.

Thus our interpretative and analytical procedure is premised on a clinical model. It is assumed that what is normal, adaptive, and constructive can be expressed in some rule of life. For example, in clinical practice it is assumed that an individual should be able to hold down a job which he wants, for which he is prepared, and at which he is a success. This rule specifies part of the content of what is meant by normality. However, there are individuals who are made anxious by the prospect of success. They become depressed and engage in activities unconsciously aimed at frustrating their achievement. The depressive reaction and the inappropriate behaviour can then be identified as abnormal, not only by general standards of life but also in terms of the aims and capacities of the individual himself as recognized by him. Rules of law or typical procedures are to this study of the jury what criteria of normality are to the clinical investigation of individuals.[6]

I will now examine five psychoanalytic principles and apply them specifically to the performance of the jury relative to some rule of law, of evidence, or of practice. The five principles do not provide a summary of psychoanalytic theory. They have been selected because of their applicability to specific psychological issues that are likely to arise for jurors and, consequently, for the insight they provide into certain important psychodynamic aspects of trials.[7]

THE PRINCIPLE OF UNCONSCIOUS MOTIVATION

Educated people are now familiar with the fact that neurotic symptoms are

6 The concepts of normal and abnormal used here are not the same as their clinical counterparts by which abnormal connotes the presence of a neurosis or a psychosis. Abnormal here connotes only the temporary disturbance of a mental process. The question of the mental stability of jurors is important in itself, given that one person in every five is likely to suffer from a significantly impairing neurosis or psychosis, although psychosis is relatively infrequent. See Hanly *Mental Health in Ontario* (1970) 4, 11.

7 Glanville Williams has analysed the intellectual and other conscious difficulties under which many jurors find themselves, such as boredom, reluctance to serve, difficulty in following complex and conflicting evidence over many days, etc. (Supra note 5, at 271). All the factors identified by Williams would tend not only to facilitate but also to reinforce the psychological factors identified in this paper.

psychogenetic, that, for example, frigidity in women or impotence in men originates in psychic conflicts unknown to the individuals who suffer them. What is not so generally appreciated is that unconscious mental processes take place in all persons and make their influence felt in a variety of ways – psychological errors, dreams, periodic mild depression, irrational attitudes, unrealistic beliefs, convictions, opinions, and values, distorted self-images, and distorted images and perceptions of others. Unconscious mental processes thus make their influence felt in the lives of individuals lacking any significant neurotic symptoms.[8] Everyone dreams; yet the dreamer's waking thoughts have usually no access to anything but the disguised manifest images and affects of the dream should it even be recalled in waking hours. The source and significance of the dream remains a mystery. Similarly, if an individual is convinced that an accused person is guilty or not guilty of a crime, the reasons he presents to himself for coming to this conclusion may disguise the thoughts and feelings that have actually caused him to be thus convinced. Consequently, in order to examine the *Truscott* trial from a psychoanalytic point of view it is not necessary to assume or seek to establish that there was anything peculiarly neurotic about the *Truscott* jurors. It is only necessary to assume that their frailties were the garden variety frailties of mankind. What is certain is that any person called to do jury duty will bring with him his own unconscious mental life and its influence may disturb his work as a juror.

In his preliminary instructions to the jury, the judge enjoins its members to remove from their minds anything they may have heard or thought about the crime or the accused so that they can base their finding on the evidence presented to the court and on nothing else. This instruction is the expression of a legal ideal for which there is an obvious justification. But the law appears to be naïve in its confidence that this rule can be carried out in practice. In this respect, the law seems to be based on prepsychoanalytic concepts of mental functioning dating from seventeenth- and eighteenth-century rationalism: the reasonable man can, by an act of will, make his mind a tabula rasa for the purpose of giving objective consideration to any matter. To be sure, given the psychological role of the judge as auxiliary superego, the judge's admonition to banish previous information and ideas about the crime will provide a powerful motive to comply. But such a motivation is already in danger of compromising the capacity of jurors to form an independent opinion. Compliance may take the form of a temporary repression of the juror's pretrial reactions, ideas, and speculations; but

8 Freud's famous study 'The Psychopathology of Everyday Life,' 6 *S.E.*, provides a detailed examination of unconscious mental functioning in the lives of normal people.

it does not follow that they will have no influence upon his evaluation of what is presented at the trial, only that he will not be aware of their influence.

THE PRINCIPLE OF HOMEOSTATIC BALANCE

The human mental organism is subject to arousal into activity by stimuli received from the environment via the senses and by sources from within itself as a result of the spontaneous action of the instincts. Once aroused, the mental organism has the task of resolving the arousal through gratification. Gratification may occur at once or be delayed; it may be direct and related to the object actually desired, or indirect and related to a substitute object as a result of the action of a defence mechanism. Dreams, for example, provide deferred substitute gratifications for wishes that are formed during waking hours but which cannot be gratified because the gratificatory behaviour would be in conflict with reality or with social or personal ethical norms. Thus, even in its sleeping state the mind is actively at work preserving its impulse life at tolerable levels of excitation (homeostatic balance) by the resolution of states of arousal. Correspondingly, it is important to understand that the human mind is always silently at work quite independently of the conscious will, even though the individual may have as part of his self-image the, to him, self-evident belief that his will is the unique sovereign of his own thoughts, feelings, fantasies, motives, and actions.

In the trial of a person accused of a violent crime, jurors are going to be subject to a series of powerfully provocative stimuli. Long before he has been called to jury duty the news of the crime will have made its impact on the prospective juror. Then, as a juror, he will be subjected to a fresh set of emotionally charged experiences; he will see the accused and be charged with the task of deciding his guilt or innocence. The courtroom and the appearance of the robed judge seated above the court are likely to be strange and impressive, if not somewhat awesome, to many jurors. During the trial, jurors are subjected to a severe restriction. They have only one significant act to perform – to decide the innocence or guilt of the accused; otherwise they are supposed to be attentive, objective observers and thoughtful analysts of the events, testimony, and rulings unfolding before them in the courtroom. And at the same time, until very recently at least, jurors have been cut off from their usual forms of intimate and recreational companionship which they would normally use to assist themselves in resolving highly charged emotional states and in working out successful adaptations to novel, demanding experiences.

Some of these factors will be considered later in the rather different contexts provided by other psychoanalytic principles, although they could also be appropriately discussed here. But perhaps two factors, the appearance of the lawyers (as distinct from their legal arguments) and the practice of sequestering, sufficiently clarify the implications of the principle of homeostatic balance for our understanding of the psychology of the trial process.

The appearance of the lawyers may influence the outcome of the trial. The jurors interviewed had retained a vivid impression of the courtroom style of the two lawyers. The jurors saw the crown attorney as a rather bumbling, awkward individual, without much experience in the courtroom or its rules of procedure but shrewd and persistent in presenting his case despite having to be corrected by the judge on numerous occasions. They felt, without being able to explain precisely why, the crown attorney was, despite his numerous courtroom errors, somehow very astute. In this the jurors were right, although the lawyer in question did not deliberately set out to achieve this effect. His behaviour enabled the jurors to identify with him even though this was not his conscious aim. They saw the defence counsel as a masterful, clever, experienced individual who could dominate witnesses, the courtroom, and the jurors. Although all the jurors avowed that if they were in trouble with the law they would want his services, nevertheless they identified with the crown counsel, and at least one juror developed a strong animosity toward the counsel for the accused, sometimes wanting to reach out of the jury box and throttle him. However brilliant a lawyer's arguments may be on behalf of the accused, it is unlikely that they will carry conviction with a juror who feels such hostility toward the individual making the defence. In the pursuit of their own narcissistic gratifications, lawyers can evidently generate dramatics in the courtroom that vie successfully with the evidence they present for influence over jurors' minds. Paradoxically, the very events during the trial that may have caused the crown attorney secretly to fear that he was not effectively presenting the case for the crown were precisely occurrences that benefited his case by facilitating identification with him by jurors who felt themselves in a similar position.

Jurors will also be affected by the fact that they are sequestered and hence cut off from relationships and actions they would normally use to reduce anxiety and resolve feelings of anger, hostility, and excessive pity and so be able to maintain a high level of tolerance for uncertainty, which is the attitude of mind required for objectivity. And, to make matters worse, if jurors are sequestered for a lengthy period of time they may become subject to some degree of instinctual regression. Indeed, the *Truscott* jurors interviewed all complained about sequestration. They felt imprisoned, frustrated by being unable to expose themselves to any sights, activities, or interests other than the trial. They were thrown into a dependency on each other in order to provide some relief from the burden of responsibility under which they laboured. Sequestering juries subjects them to a psychological predicament and also promotes a group identification that is itself usually regressive since it reduces the capacity of the individual to observe and think for himself and thus form his own opinion concerning the guilt or innocence of the accused.

Since the time of the *Truscott* trial, the federal Parliament has wisely recognized the need to assist jurors with this difficulty.[9] In order to protect jurors from external influence during the crucial stage of their deliberation, juries must remain sequestered after they have received their charge. But during the course of a long trial the judge may allow jurors to return to their homes during periods of adjournment. The trial judge is now responsible for weighing the hazards of a long period of isolation against the risk of extraneous influences upon the objectivity of jurors. The wise use of this discretion could go a long way toward removing the psychological liabilities of sequestration. Nevertheless, it remains true that isolation will place an unusually heavy burden on jurors for the resolution of conflicting psychic demands. The courts should be aware of this problem and do everything possible to ease it. Otherwise the judgment of jurors may be disturbed by their subjective reactions to the trial either in the direction of a sentimental acquittal or in the direction of a vindictive finding of guilt.

THE PRINCIPLE OF INFANTILE SEXUALITY

The instincts themselves impose severe demands upon the mental organism for homeostatic resolution. The instincts develop derivative impulses, aims, behavioural modes of gratification, and ideational representation according to the major stages (phases) through which they pass in the course of individual physical and mental development. An important aspect of this development for the purposes of this paper is the universal tendency in small children to confuse sexual intercourse with violence when they observe it or fantasize it. This perception of sexuality is typi-

9 Section 576 of the Criminal Code was amended in 1972 to provide that the 'judge may, at any time before the jury retires to consider its verdict, permit the members of the jury to separate.' Previously the judge could not allow the members of the jury to separate during the trial of a capital offence.

cally repressed along with the repression of the Oedipus complex itself at the onset of the latency period (age of five or six to the onset of puberty). It is commonly aroused into activity again with puberty either as a result of impulse fixation at, or instinctual regression to, one of the infantile sexual organizations. Consequently, pubescent boys and girls fantasize, dream, and talk about intercourse as a form of violence. Three important corollaries follow. 1/ A pubescent boy is psychosexually equipped by his pre-pubescent development for acts of sexual violence. 2/ However, in the lives of almost all individuals this proclivity is not so strongly energized that it cannot be satisfied by the production of a rich fantasy life upon this theme associated with masturbation and followed by feelings of guilt. 3/ Adults, whether or not they are able to recall them, will have memories of these episodes in their own personal histories. Now, a report of a sex crime acts as a stimulus upon these unconscious memories in individuals whose adult lives are quite exemplary, giving rise to an unsettling fascination with the crime and generating in the minds of the intrigued observers the question 'Why am I so fascinated by this sordid crime?' To this question there is usually no answer because the memories of adolescence and the memories of the root experiences in the childhood of the individual which alone could yield an answer are silenced by repression.

Some jurors interviewed stated that before the trial they did have thoughts and discussions with others about the crime and the accused. They thought that he was innocent because a boy of fourteen would not be capable of doing such a thing. There is no reason to doubt the sincerity of these statements as expressions of the conscious thoughts of these jurors. Nevertheless, it is also true that the conscious thought 'a fourteen-year-old boy isn't capable of raping and strangling a girl' may be the psychological denial of just the opposite repressed thoughts. The will to believe that adolescent children are innocent of sexual and aggressive aims is the expression in conscious thought of the activity of a defence against memories of just such aims in one's own past. It is not being asserted that all pubescent boys teeter precariously on the brink of sadistic sexual crimes and that memories of this Hyde-like self are universally repressed. Psychoanalysis has shown that unconscious fantasies can function as the *psychological* equivalents of real experiences and produce in the ego a guilt or anxiety commensurate with real occurrences. Thus memory holds the key to an appreciation of the psychological potential for sadistic sexual crimes in any pubescent or adult male. A denial of this sort, if it were at work, would lay the groundwork for a subsequent projection of guilt upon the accused which could in turn exert a pressure in the direction of a finding of legal guilt. From a psychoanalytic point of view a juror could only be considered to be definitively immune to the tendency to project subjective guilt onto an accused person if he could recall, without distortion, his own adolescent and infantile sexual fantasies.

THE PRINCIPLE OF PSYCHIC DEFENCE

Psychoanalysis has identified the existence and described the operation of defence mechanisms which the psychic organism has at its disposal to maintain homeostatic balance and, in particular, to maintain anxiety at tolerable levels. Among these defence mechanisms are repression, projection, denial, sublimation, isolation, reaction-formation, and identification. Of these, four are of particular interest for this study. 'Repression' is the process which inhibits the recall of past experiences. It produces a psychogenetic amnesia, mild, temporary forms of which are familiar to everyone in the experience of being unable to recall a known name. 'Projection' is the process whereby qualities of self are attributed to something external, as when in childhood aggressive impulses are projected into some dark unfamiliar place within the home such as an attic, basement, closet, etc, so that it is 'seen' by the child to be the domicile of a hostile, threatening agency. This state of affairs is commonly referred to as childhood paranoia. 'Denial' is the process whereby some aspect of reality is 'put out of circuit' in relation to the self as though it did not exist, as when an individual strongly influenced by feelings of envy loudly protests his lack of envy and, indeed, does know nothing consciously of such feelings in himself. 'Identification' as a defence is a process whereby an individual alienates some function or responsibility from himself and assigns it to another or others to exercise on his behalf while preserving the feeling that he is still exercising it himself. The aim is protection from the anxiety of having to do some forbidding task. Political and ideological affiliations are often inherited in this way.

In general, defence mechanisms work to maintain anxiety at tolerable levels and to ward off painful recognitions. Information about the occurrence of a violent crime, for example, will arouse anxiety, especially if the person who committed it has not yet been arrested. Superadded to this realistic anxiety will be a subjectively originated anxiety, because the information will also arouse old guilt-provoking memories and fantasies into activity. Repression occurs when these memories cannot be recalled, however helpful they might be in finding a valid personal orientation toward the crime and the criminal. An example of this effect combined with projection are the rumours and gossip that quickly surround the occurrence of a sensational sex murder. In the living rooms of the area in which Lynne Harper lived one can still hear totally ungrounded speculations congenial to the unconscious fantasies of the local gossips repeated with an air of scandalized excitement.

These mental processes can also 'find' guilty an accused person who, on the courtroom evidence alone, may or may not be. Anyone charged with the responsibility of deciding on the guilt or innocence of an accused person will have to deal in some way with his own unconscious reactions to the crime. If these are guilt-provoking, there is always the danger that an impartial assessment of evidence presented for and against the accused will be impaired by an unconscious need to find the accused guilty. The defence mechanism at work in such an event would be projection, which brings about the alienation of guilt feelings from the self and their transference to the accused. In this way unconsciously determined feelings of psychological guilt can influence decisions concerning legal guilt.

The point being made here is strictly theoretical. Interviews with jurors provided no observations from which one could definitively infer the occurrence of this type of psychopathology as a major influence upon the jurors' decisions. However, one feature of the reactions of the jurors interviewed is consistent with this pattern. The jurors were naturally keenly interested in the comportment of the accused. Jurors found Truscott impassive, defiant, belligerent – 'he could stare you down' – or indifferent, except when young female witnesses appeared. Then he was observed by jurors to respond with animation, winking and smiling at the witnesses. Each juror imagined this behaviour to be that of a tough, sexually depraved youth. Some had a fantasy of him as a youthful village stud, servicing the girls of the neighbourhood as they came of age. One remarked ruefully that the accused seemed to be better endowed than himself. These ideas were not based on any evidence placed before the court; one can only treat them as fantasies. As such, they do have the distinct appearance of the return of the repressed in a form disguised by projection. To the extent that this happened, jurors would be, unknown to themselves, biased against the accused. The recognition of bias would be difficult to make because the projection would make it appear self-evident to the juror that he was perceiving the guilt of the crime in the behaviour of the accused 'plain as the palm of your hand.'

This process must be clearly differentiated from something akin to it which is perfectly appropriate in itself – observing the accused to form an impression of whether or not he is the kind of person who could commit the crime. Even these impressions are hazardous, however, because of the effects that being accused of a crime, imprisoned, and placed on trial may have on the appearance and behaviour of the accused person.

It is of interest to note how obliquely pertinent to this issue is the dissent in the *Truscott* case written by Mr Justice Emmett Hall in the Supreme Court of Canada judgment.[10] Mr Justice Hall was of the opinion that Jocelyn Godette's testimony was inappropriately led by the prosecuting counsel, whose reference to it and interpretations of it were such as to incite the jury against the accused by establishing in their minds that the accused had wanted to have sexual intercourse with the witness on the evening of the crime and, having been frustrated in that objective, turned to Lynne Harper as an alternative. However, although one of them repeated the prosecution's theory, it was evident from the interviews that the jurors were primarily impressed by the *reaction* of the accused to the *appearance* of this witness rather than by anything she said or by any construction the prosecution placed upon it. Something in this reaction aroused in the jurors a sense of the guilt of the accused, as though they felt his courtroom behaviour at this point to be precociously shameless and an implicit demonstration of guilt. It was on this perceived meaning (whether it be considered a projection or an objective perception) that the plausibility of the prosecution's case rested for the jury, not on the precise details of the evidence, the lawyer's use of it in substantiating their theories, or the judge's instructions to the jury about it. Thus the Supreme Court judges, including Mr Justice Hall, as well as the lawyers presenting the case, became involved in a complex, abstract, legal game of moves and counter-moves based on the unsubstantiated assumption that jurors follow this game with the interest and understanding with which they would follow a game of hockey. These legal debates appear to have bypassed the concrete psychological processes by which justice was done or not done in the court of law. The law, from this point of view, turns a blind eye to the real course of justice because it assumes that the outcome of a jury trial is actually decided by the evidence presented by the lawyers, their arguments, and the instructions of the judge to the jury. These form the context for the decision, but they are by no means the basis for it. A powerful play of psychological forces and reactions overlooked by the law may often have the decisive influence on the outcome.

These considerations bear on one of the legal issues raised by the *Truscott* trial. Should defence counsel have sought a change of venue for the trial? Mrs LeBourdais strongly suggests in her examination of the trial that Mr Donnelly, the defence lawyer, who was himself born and raised in the county, was naïve in thinking that there was not a sufficient risk of prejudice against his client to justify the costs to the defendant's family of a change of venue.[11] A change of venue cannot remove the risk of emotional prejudice against someone accused of a violent sexual crime. Jurors in any part of the province would have to deal with their own unconscious reactions to the crime and the accused. But a change of venue might have removed two potential obstacles to an unbiased trial.

1/ The members of the community (any community) in which such a crime takes place are likely to be stimulated to form fixed opinions about the accused prior to a trial by the circulation of information and misinformation within the community itself. The immediate community will be in a higher state of excitement about it and for a longer period than remote communities. This generalization holds even if most of the *Truscott* jurors were, as they claimed in interviews to have been, quite unoccupied by the crime over the summer for reasons peculiar to each until they were reminded of it by being called to jury duty.

2/ In this case the accused was also a member of a distinct group within the county – the air force personnel and their families. There develops an extended kinship bond among members of a community who are born into it, raised within it, and share in a common way of life – here, that of an agricultural community. The psychological basis of this kinship bond is a common identification animated by a libidinal tie which in turn is protected by the projection of hostile feelings onto an alien group.[12] This kinship is fissured in many places by religion, politics, ethnic origin, and intra-community vocational differentiation, but these splits can easily diminish in significance when a community is faced with the prospect of a violent criminal in its midst. The permanent members of the community will want to believe that the guilty person is not one of them. This wish, combining with the projection of unconscious hostile impulses onto the 'outsiders' in their midst, causes a desire to believe one of the 'outsiders' guilty. Hence many members of this rural community would have heaved a sigh of relief when someone from the air force base was accused of the crime. And

11 LeBourdais, supra note 3 at 51
12 For an elaborated psychoanalytic theory of group dynamics see Freud, 'Group Psychology and the Analysis of the Ego,' (1955), 18 *S.E.* at 100–4. The supplementary assumption made here is that a common way of life, heritage, work, etc, can act as a substitute for a common leader in the formation of a relatively weak yet substantial and stable group identity.

projected hostility would cause these same people to relish any fact or fantasy pointing in the direction of his guilt. But members of this community were not bereft of conscience or of the capacity to discriminate fact from fiction. And not a few members of the community had associated with air force families and formed friendships with them. This was particularly true of townspeople in the community. One would be committing the logical fallacy of division in attempting to deduce anything about the attitudes of particular individuals from this demonstrable group phenomenon. My own impression, based on interviews with jurors, is that they did, to a substantial degree, function as individuals, and as individuals they denied the validity of the allegation of bias against the accused suggested by Mrs LeBourdais. One juror, for instance, had close associations with air force personnel at another military base in the community. However, the possibility of 'projection' does provide an argument in favour of a change of venue in such cases.

Two useful conclusions can be drawn from these considerations: a change of venue cannot be expected to solve all of the psychological problems generated for jurors in the trial of an individual accused of a violent sexual crime; nevertheless, defence attorneys should give careful consideration to the problem of community bias in such cases.

THE PRINCIPLE OF SUPEREGO MENTAL GOVERNANCE

The superego is a set of unconscious functions and contents with the ego itself.[13] These functions determine the moral and aesthetic responses of the individual. They are themselves governed by introjected parental images and admonitions. It is the superego that makes self-condemnation possible. It is the superego that punishes the ego with guilt when it fails to fulfil the demands of its imperatives. And it is the superego that requires the repression of impulses and wishes that demand gratification through morally or aesthetically unacceptable forms of behaviour. Just as the instinctual unconscious is the source of fascination with a sensational crime, so the superego is the source of the reaction of moral horror to it.

Individuals often find it difficult to tolerate the burden of superego

13 For a comprehensive statement of this and the above principles consult Freud, 'Three Essays on Sexuality,' 7 S.E.; 'Introductory Lectures on Psycho-analysis,' (1963), 15–16 S.E.; 'The Ego and the Id,' (1961), 19 S.E.; 'Inhibitions, Symptoms and Anxiety,' (1961), 20 S.E.; Anna Freud The Ego and the Mechanisms of Defence (1948); Brenner An Elementary Textbook of Psychoanalysis (1957).

functioning. Consequently, they are content to enter into groups through which they can form a common identificatory idealization of a single individual to whom is assigned the role of providing moral leadership to the group. Religious organizations work in this way. And so do courts. The judge is the superego of the judicial process.[14] The lawyers are to set out the facts, and the jury must find on them, but the judge regulates their presentation, decides what may or may not be admitted, and generally imposes order on the proceedings. Most importantly, it is for the judge to pronounce sentence. The language and the formalities of courtroom observance and even the architecture and furniture of the courtroom are designed to emphasize the superego role of the judge and enhance his awesomeness. This psychological role gives the judge a very great potential for influence upon the jury. To the authority of fact and reason and his knowledge of the law there is added the psychological authority of an auxiliary superego. Consequently, it must also be understood that the judge can direct a jury psychologically as well as legally and his psychological directions may be inappropriate, though his legal directions may be unexceptionable.

The role of the judge is therefore crucial. The preconditions for the psychological formation described above reside in the inevitable unfamiliarity of jurors with courts, court proceedings, and the law, combined with the authority the judge must exercise in all matters of law. He is the man whose decisions bind the conduct of the clever, highly educated, and well-to-do lawyers who contest the case for the crown and the accused. In the court his word is law. His rulings may be challenged, but he alone decides whether to uphold or alter his ruling.

The judge of the *Truscott* trial was seen by the jurors as an awesome figure. They spoke of him in terms of reverential respect. One juror recalled his surprise at finding the judge to be so impressive and stated that he had not expected to have this feeling. This means that the jurors, in addition to being consciously attuned to the instructions and admonitions of the judge, will have been unconsciously attuned to any slight, implicit, non-verbal as well as verbal communications bearing on the judge's opinion concerning the guilt or innocence of the accused.

It is, of course, true that the jury alone bears the responsibility for deciding guilt or innocence. The judge instructs the jury very carefully on this point. But the instruction concerning the law is at odds in this respect

14 For a discussion of the judge as a parent figure see Schoenfeld supra note 1, at 16.

with the psychology of his role under the law in the courtroom.[15] Hence jurors are likely to experience a conflict within themselves between the verbal instruction and the non-verbal psychological identity and function of the judge. It is not inconceivable that his role identity in the mind of the juror may have a greater influence upon the thinking of the juror than his words.

Some of the *Truscott* jurors, at least, developed an interest in the judge's opinion of the guilt or innocence of the accused during the progress of the trial. One juror felt that sometimes when the lawyers were arguing about technical legal points the judge would be miles away figuring it out (Truscott's guilt or innocence). He, the judge, knew the truth. Another juror felt the judge was impartial throughout and gave no sign of believing the accused guilty or innocent until his charge to the jury. Then this juror felt that the judge had concluded that the accused was guilty. Another juror felt uncertain about the judge's attitude – sometimes he felt the judge thought Truscott guilty – at other times he did not know. However, when the jury had to go back for further instruction about part of the evidence and the judge was giving his instruction, the juror was sure that the judge thought the accused was guilty. At this point the defence counsel objected, and the judge decided to have the portion of evidence read from the court record. In terms of the law, nothing had gone amiss; the defence objection had been accepted, and the record had been read. However, the law does not take into account the effects of silent, unconscious processes in the minds of the jury which may be much more influential in forming a juror's opinion than the explicit verbal content of the courtroom procedure. An unconscious thought process may be at work along the following lines: 'the judge thinks the accused guilty; if the judge thinks so, it must be so.' This cogitation need never become conscious in the mind of the juror. From the 'security' of the superego, it can influence the juror's assessment and appreciation of everything that has gone on in the court.

This influence is by no means limited to specific events of the obvious type mentioned above, such as when the judge is perceived by a juror to be giving a tendentious reading of the evidence. An examination of the trans-

15 Glanville Williams makes the point, supra note 5, at 304, that 'the judge must not use such language as to lead the jury to think that he is directing them that they must find the facts in the way that he indicates.' He goes on to add, 'Quite apart from any expression of opinion by the judge, the way in which he marshals the facts and gets rid of irrelevancies may present a strongly persuasive argument for one side or the other.' To this apt formulation our analysis must add that the judge may be quite unaware of the nature and extent of his influence because it is not only the legal and factual content of his summing up that signifies to the juror but also the manner of his doing so.

cript of the *Truscott* trial reveals several examples of this influence, the significance and importance of which psychoanalysis has enabled us to understand and more thoroughly appreciate. In his communications to the jury, the judge appealed to superego-derived attitudes in the jurors when referring to their assessment of the evidence pointing to the guilt of the accused. For example, 'you must not permit the fact of his youth in any way to prevent you from bringing in a verdict in accordance with your *conscience*. Nor, on the other hand, ought you to allow the *revolting nature of the facts* surrounding this case in any way to influence you to bring in a verdict which is, in any way, shape or form, *contrary to the evidence*, or based on anything but the evidence ... if the evidence raises a doubt in your mind, you will acquit him. When I say raises a doubt in your mind, I mean a reasonable doubt. Not a foolish doubt or a doubt because you are hesitant about doing your duty, and I am sure I need not say to a Jury of the County of Huron that I know you will accept your responsibilities in this matter, come what may, and that you will bring in a verdict according to your *conscience*.' Earlier, in the charge to them, the jury had been told: 'your churches may be the lid of respectability in the community but you, Gentlemen of the Jury, are the barometer of that respectability. You are the screws that hold the lid down and in place. The whole character of your community depends on the way you do your *duty* in this case.'[16]

With unconscious precision, the judge associated finding the accused guilty with the performance of duty according to conscience. The last sentence was especially provocative without his consciously intending it to be so, because it evoked the theme of the goodness and safety of the community, suggesting to the juror the question, 'would you want that boy living next door to your little girl?'

In contrast, the judge addressed the jurors' ego attitudes and feelings when referring to their assessment of the evidence pointing to the innocence of the accused. The jurors were cautioned, quite rightly, not to let the unpleasantness of the facts interfere with an impartial assessment of them and their implications. But embedded in his communications there is the unconscious assertion, 'what is moral in you will find the accused guilty.' Such a thought will communicate itself to a jury without their being aware that they have received it or recognizing its influence upon their thinking. It would be felt only as a vague yet potent anxiety bound to the thought that it would be wrong not to find the accused guilty.

16 My emphasis. The judge's charge is reproduced in Friedland *Cases and Materials on Criminal Law and Procedure* (4th ed, 1974) at 761.

In a slip of the tongue, the judge quite possibly revealed his private opinion that the accused was guilty: 'If, after you have decided in your minds what the facts are, you can think of any rational explanation of them inconsistent with the prisoner's innocence – I should say, inconsistent with the prisoner's guilt; or indeed, if you have any doubt about it, you must acquit him.' The interfering repressed thought would appear to be the negative of the thought consciously uttered: 'It will be hard for you to find a rational explanation of the facts inconsistent with his guilt.' The jurors would have pre-consciously detected the significance of this slip and been influenced by it. Writers from the earliest times employed psychological errors to communicate facets of the motives, feelings, and thoughts of heroes and heroines of which they were not yet aware. Jurors can be likened in this respect to the spectators at a dramatic performance.

We have already considered the importance of the witness Jocelyn Godette and the crown's interpretation that the accused was planning to rape and kill her. The judge took a special interest in the testimony of this witness.

HAYES Q Was there any more conversation between you then, on Tuesday?

A Well, he just kept on telling me to 'don't tell anybody to come with you, and that is all.'

HIS LORDSHIP Q Say that again. He just kept on telling me what?

A Not to tell anybody.

Mr Justice Emmett Hall of the Supreme Court fastened on this episode in his minority opinion, claiming that it contributed to misguiding the jury as to the import of the evidence and in such a way as to prejudice them against the accused. In fixing on this point, Mr Justice Hall was being guided by a sure, if uninformed, feeling for the kind of factor we have been considering. A wise judge is like an intuitive creative writer: he has an instinctive prescientific sense of the workings of unconscious mental forces.

The judge's role is particularly important in the way he interprets the court procedures for the jury. Jurors usually have very little knowledge of the legal process. Consider the problem that arose in the *Truscott* trial when the crown attorney in his opening remarks made reference to a statement taken from the accused but not admitted as evidence. This situation left jurors knowing that the accused had made a statement but without knowing what it contained – whether it was a confession or not. (Jurors who followed the subsequent controversy would have read that the statement was not a confession.) Some of the jurors interviewed stated that they were left at the time of the trial in a state of uncertainty about it and had followed the instruction to disregard it. However, at least one juror did believe that it was a confession, it was not admitted because it was not in the interest of the accused to have it presented to the jury, and the court was protecting the interest of the accused. But this juror also stated that he had followed the judge's instruction and disregarded it in reaching his conclusion. The question is whether or not jurors are really able to resist being influenced by opinions of this kind in reaching a verdict. Yet another juror stated that he had no thought of the statement's being a confession, but in another context indicated that evidence rejected by the judge must be damaging.

This issue points to a psychological difficulty many jurors must encounter as a result of not being familiar with the rules of evidence. When a person is deprived of an objective frame of reference in which to place an experience, that experience will still be interpreted, and there is every likelihood that it will be interpreted subjectively. For example, one of the jurors felt that the statement must not have been a confession because a confession would have made a trial unnecessary. In other words he felt under a psychological constraint to form some interpretation of the significance of the statement.

This compulsion to interpret is readily understood from a psychoanalytic point of view. For example, when the mind is subjected to a stimulus during sleep (e.g. a loud or unusual noise) and the sleeper is not aroused by it to form an objective opinion of its nature and source, the unconscious life of the sleeper will produce a dream which provides a context in its manifest content for the interpretation of the stimulus. Similarly, the mind of ancient man, in the absence of an objective understanding of natural phenomena such as plagues, assigned to them the significance of divine retribution provoked by the presence in their midst of an unexpiated crime. The unconscious life of modern man still obeys the compulsion to interpret. The jurors' predicament in this situation may be likened to that of the sleeper or the ancient. Like the sleeper who is deprived of perceptions of reality by his sleeping state, the juror is denied access to reality by the rules of evidence, i.e. in the *Truscott* case to the statement made by the accused. Like the ancient, whose mind was not educated in a scientific frame of reference for understanding nature, the juror has to function without a thorough grounding in the law of trials. Consequently, his thinking is deprived of the two best defences against the formation of opinions produced by subjective thinking, which is peculiarly vulnerable to unconscious determination. The only objective indications a juror had, in the case under consideration, are the fact that the prosecution made reference to the statement and the fact that it is the task of the prosecution to present evidence establishing the guilt of the accused. These indicators would tend to open the door to the idea that there must be something damaging to the accused in the suppressed material. The other defence available to the juror is the moral authority of the judge on behalf of the prohibition against considering the matter at all. Unfortunately, this moral authority can easily be undermined by the thought that the judge is doing his best to protect the interest of the accused. This is surely itself a distorted impression of the judge's work, which is to make sure that the trial is impartial, that is, that the rules of evidence are scrupulously observed. The distortion arises out of the need to see the judge as a person who will do everything he can for a guilty person. This need to so perceive the judge is likely to arise in the mind of any juror who is himself subject to guilt-arousing unconscious memories. That is to say we are not dealing here with the objective meaning of the judge's actions but with their subjective significance to a juror. This notion, when combined in the juror's mind with the further impression that the judge believes the accused is guilty, may disarm the juror's determination to make his own assessment of the evidence and cause him to underestimate the importance and significance of defence testimony.

CONCLUSIONS

There is no reason to think that the *Truscott* jurors functioned any differently than jurors generally. There is no reason to be particularly critical of them. However, there is reason to believe that psychopathological factors were at work then and usually are at work in trials beneath the legal exchanges. How, then, can trial procedures be altered in order to assist jurors in carrying out their duties with a minimum of disturbance from those psychopathological factors?

The present study indicates a number of possibilities.

1 The members of the jury could be drawn from a pool of experts trained to perform the jury function and to deal with the emotional factors that may disturb judgment.[17] This reform would also have the advantage that juries could be drawn from persons who had no close connection with the

17 Glanville Williams discusses legal reforms of this type, supra note 5, at 298.

community in which the crime was committed and thus avoid the potential for bias against the accused.

2 Juries could be selected as they now are and thoroughly briefed by a legal expert on courtroom procedures, rules of evidence, and the like, so that they would have an objective frame of reference in which to place and assess the significance of various events in the courtroom. This falls under the rubric of ego-strengthening, assisting the jury to develop and use rational, legally informed attitudes in carrying out their work. In addition, judges could deal explicitly with these issues as they arise, telling the jury how the situation should be understood and what weight should be given to it.

3 Legal aid should provide assistance to those who are unable to meet the additional costs involved in a change of venue in order to eliminate a financial constraint against seeking this remedy when it is thought to be useful in ensuring a fair trial.

4 When a trial is likely to be long, judges should consider carefully the possibility of allowing jurors to return home overnight and/or on weekends during the course of the trial.

5 Judges could learn to deal explicitly with emotionally charged fantasies likely to prey on jurors in the context of a trial – something that would tend to neutralize their influence upon a juror's decision.

6 Judges could refrain from making highly charged moralistic statements, especially if they are tendentious by association. In general, the more the judge is able himself to be dispassionate about the case, the more he will be able to serve as a model of rational objectivity for the jury rather than as an auxiliary superego.

7 Trial lawyers could learn to identify and deal explicitly with psychological factors in the trial which may be unduly influencing the jurors. If there is danger of the unconscious projection of guilt onto the accused, it may be offset or minimized by explicit tactful statements by the defence attorney or by the judge.

8 Perhaps as a first step, trial lawyers could struggle to adopt a less gladiatorial attitude to each other in the court room and allow emphasis to be focussed on the facts and the legal issues rather than on their own egos.

9 And finally, judges could be expected to acquire a greater measure of insight into the psychological factors that may disturb the judicial process. The acquisition of such insight would ensure that their crucial role in judicial proceedings would not be subject to psychopathology; they would be able to identify and deal with psychopathological disturbance of the

judicial process in the courtroom and could serve as a model to the other participants. A not insignificant secondary benefit of such knowledge and insight would be an enhanced ability to appreciate psychiatric testimony both during a trial and in sentencing.[18]

Psychoanalytic knowledge, both in the study and evaluation of judicial processes and in the administration of justice in our courts, would be of great use to the Canadian judicial system.

CHARLES HANLY, a graduate of the University of Toronto, is an associate professor in the Department of Philosophy, University of Toronto. He is a member of the Canadian Psychoanalytic Society and conducts a part-time practice in psycho-analysis. His books include a study for the Ontario Committee on the Healing Arts, *Mental Health in Ontario* (1970), and *Psychoanalysis and Philosophy* (1970).

18 Jerome Frank has recommended that 'each prospective judge should undergo something like a psychoanalysis ... Such self-knowledge ... can be of immense help in reducing the consequences of judicial bias' (supra note 1, at 250). See Schoenfeld, supra note 1, at 16.

PETER RUSSELL

Judicial power in Canada's political culture

Perhaps I am overly self-conscious, but I must confess to a certain sense of
unease when I refer to 'judicial power' in Canada. Such talk, I suspect, will
be regarded by most of my political science colleagues as irrelevant or
trivial, by members of the legal profession as misguided and ill-informed,
and by at least some of our public leaders as socially dangerous (if not
obscene). But as a political scientist I find it impossible to leave the subject
alone. I have long been fascinated with the phenomenon of judicial power
in different societies, but especially in our own. It is (or has been) such
quiet power, so unacclaimed, so often denied! It is precisely the subtle,
ironic, strength which our judiciary derives from its hidden nature that so
fascinates me.

   Now a scientific political scientist should at this point trot out a tidy little
definition of 'power' which could be 'operationalized' so that all could
identify, and even measure objectively, Canadian judicial power. I never
learned to do political science that way, so I can only offer this notion of the
power that interests me: the initiation of significant changes in our customs,
our laws, or institutions and the maintenance of some important features of
the established order. Our judiciary clearly has the power to do these
things. What I wish to discuss here is our changing perceptions of this
power and the way in which these perceptions may influence that power.

   I can think of no better place to begin a discussion of judicial power in
Canada than at the point where it first struck me as such an intriguing
element in our system of government. That is, when I came across the
following words in a judicial opinion: 'It is, in fact, a prime element in the

self-government of the Dominion, that it should be able to secure through its own courts of justice that the law should be one and the same for all its citizens.'[1] Now these words would not raise an eyebrow if uttered in the context of a unitary state such as England. But they were not; the Dominion referred to, the Dominion through whose courts the law should 'be one and the same for all its citizens,' was Canada, a federal country.

The quoted words are Lord Jowitt's and they formed part of the Judicial Committee of the Privy Council's 1947 decision that upheld, as constitutionally valid, federal legislation making the Supreme Court of Canada the exclusive final Court of Appeal for all Canadian courts in all matters of Canadian law, federal and provincial. These words, in effect, declared that Canada must have a unitary judicial system. These words were, in fact, quite unnecessary for the judgment at hand.[2] But it is interesting that these words were uttered as such a light-hearted reference to the apparently self-evident fact that Canada must have a unitary judicial system. It is interesting because these words were uttered by the very court that for three-quarters of a century had presided with such tender, loving care over the division of legislative powers in Canadian federalism and in the process had done its level best (by upholding provincial legislation and striking down federal legislation) to ensure that the law would *not* be one and the same for all Canadians.

The question arises how a tribunal which cared so much about Canada's having a federal division of legislative powers could be so off-hand about its having a unitary judicial system? This question becomes more intriguing when one compares Canada with the United States, where the situation is almost completely reversed. There, the national Supreme Court, while promoting a centralization of legislative power, has, especially since *Erie Railroad* v *Tompkins*,[3] been careful to respect state judicial autonomy in legal matters subject to local legislative authority.

The key to the Canadian situation is, I think, the relative innocence about judicial power which prevailed here for so long. If courts do not in any significant sense legislate, then there is no reason why devotees of federalism should be concerned about the division of judicial power. For, in essence, courts have no power. To quote my own rendition of the logic of this thinking from an earlier article: 'Courts administer justice – legisla-

---

1 *A.-G. Ont.* v *A.-G. Can.*, [1947] A.C. 127, at 154
2 The decision was based primarily on certain implications of the Statute of Westminster and an earlier decision giving the broadest possible meaning to the federal parliament's power under s 101 of the BNA Act to provide for a general court of appeal for Canada.
3 (1938) 304 U.S. 64

tures exercise power – federalism has to do with dividing power, not justice – *ergo*, the Supreme Court's jurisdiction need not be federalized.'[4] It may well have been a good thing that this innocence about judicial power (or this cunning disguise) prevailed in Canadian legal thought for so long. For it may be argued that it enabled the Supreme Court and the Judicial Committee of the Privy Council to have a unifying effect on Canadian law and thereby partially offset the centrifugal influence these courts had on legislative power in Canada.[5]

But I am not concerned with that issue here. In the present context what interests me is that this innocence about judicial power has not continued to characterize legal thinking in Canada. In the quarter century since Lord Jowitt's words were uttered, the mask has been, at least in part, removed. The undermining of the legal intelligentsia's belief in the non-political, mechanistic nature of judicial decision-making was stimulated by the drive for judicial self-government in the thirties and forties. As is well known, this movement was sparked by Canadian criticism of the way in which their lordships of the Privy Council had interpreted the Canadian constitution, the BNA Act. At first, the criticism tended to take the line that the Judicial Committee had erred in a purely legal sense and, to use the language of the 1939 *O'Connor Report* to the Canadian Senate, charged that there had been 'most serious and persistent deviation on the part of the Judicial Committee from the actual text of the Act.'[6] But fairly soon the argument shifted to more avowedly political contentions, emphasizing the need to have a final court of appeal which 'would be a better agency of constitutional adaptation.'[7] Canadian judges would, it was claimed, display a greater sensitivity to the needs of the country in serving as the final judicial arbiters of its constitutional law.

But once the case for judicial self-government shifts to these grounds, it concedes that in the judicial application of laws men make a difference and judicial decisions are not mechanically deduced from previously established rules of law. Following the attainment of judicial autonomy in 1949, there was evidence that these new currents of judicial realism in Canada

---

4 Russell, 'The Jurisdiction of the Supreme Court of Canada: Present Policies and a Programme for Reform,' (1968), 6 *Osg. Hall L. J.* 1, at 5
5 For a statement on the Supreme Court's and the Privy Council's potential for unifying Canadian law, see Willis, 'Securing Uniformity of Law in a Federal System,' (1943–4), 5 *U.T.L.J.* 352.
6 Senate of Canada *Report to the Honourable the Speaker Relating to the Enactment of the BNA Act, 1867* (1939), at 11
7 MacDonald, 'The Constitution in a Changing World,' (1948), 26 *Can. Bar Rev.* 21, at 45

would not be confined to constitutional law. In the legal periodicals, writers such as Horace Read, Gilbert Kennedy, and Bora Laskin[8] began to urge Canada's senior appellate courts to take a 'more Canadian' approach to the common law and important facets of statutory interpretation. Canadian judicial nationalism began to evoke echoes of provincial judicial nationalism from Quebec. Just as nationalist Canadian jurists denounced the British judges for their insensitive interpretation of the Canadian constitution, nationalist lawyers in Quebec resumed their protest against the Supreme Court of Canada's insensitive interpretation of Quebec's Civil Code and Code of Procedure.[9] It is remarkable that the prominent Canadian judicial nationalists, men such as Frank Scott, V.C. MacDonald, and Bora Laskin, have shown little sympathy for this provincial echo of their own refrain. But they may yet learn, as indeed the current crop of Canadian economic nationalists is learning, that, like it or not, one kind of nationalism begets another.

Quebec reaction to the new realism in Canadian legal thought is one indication that an increased acknowledgment of judicial power may lead to a lessening of judicial authority. Certainly Canadian legal scholars have been more diffident and cautious in their expressions of realism than their American counterparts. As with so many intellectual trends which originate south of the border, judicial realism arrived in Canada a decade or so after its emergence in the United States. This time lag at least has the advantage of enabling Canadians to avoid the excesses of enthusiasm for or opposition to these new intellectual trends. In this case there were few, if any, counterparts to American extremists who are inclined to treat the judiciary as simply a specialized branch of the legislature – as if appellate judges simply translate their whims into judicial findings.[10] Writers such as Frank Scott, Wolfgang Friedmann, Bora Laskin, Mark MacGuigan, and Paul Weiler, while acknowledging the important 'policy-making' role of appeal courts, have taken pains to emphasize the distinctive characteristics

---

8 Read, 'The Judicial Process in Common Law in Canada,' (1959), 37 *Can. Bar Rev.* 265; Kennedy, 'Supreme Court of Canada – *Stare Decisis* – Role of Canada's Final Court,' (1955), 33 *Can. Bar Rev.* 340 and 630; Laskin, 'The Supreme Court of Canada: A Final Court of and for Canadians,' (1951), 29 *Can. Bar Rev.* 1038

9 See, for instance, Quebec *Report of Royal Commission of Inquiry on Constitutional Problems* ('Tremblay Report') (1956), esp. III, part 5, bk I, ch *10*. For an account of this protest movement earlier in Canadian history, see Russell *The Supreme Court of Canada as a Bilingual and Bicultural Institution* (1969).

10 See, for example, Rodell *Nine Men: A Political History of the Supreme Court from 1790 to 1955* (1955), or Dahl *A Preface to Democratic Theory* (1956).

of this exercise of judicial discretion.[11] This interpretation has emphasized that judicial lawmaking is interstitial, that it occurs, ideally, in the setting of the adjudicative process, so that the parties to the legal controversy rather than the judges raise the issues and develop the contending arguments, and that it takes the form of reasoned arguments based on legal doctrines and precedents.

Now, in all of this we can see, I think, a shrewd political instinct. For these writers and others who decry political analyses of judicial behaviour sense that the legitimacy of the courts, and in particular the legitimacy of our Supreme Court acting as the nation's highest constitutional arbiter, may depend to a large degree on a very unrealistic image of the judicial role. In a democratic age, recognized authority to make laws and initiate policy is not readily conferred on an appointed judiciary. As I have suggested elsewhere, the position of our judges is analogous 'to that of the monarchy facing the advance of parliamentary democracy: they could best retain popular respect by denying that they exercised real power. But unlike monarchy, myth and reality in the judges' case have remained too far apart.'[12] It is unlikely that as the public become more sophisticated about the realities of the judicial process, judicial power can continue to shelter behind the mask of an ideology which denies the very existence of that power.

In the United States, with a constitutional doctrine emphasizing checks and balances rather than parliamentary supremacy, judicial realism has been more compatible with the popular political culture. In some states there is a tradition of elected judges which underlines the political power entailed in judging; the process of selecting Supreme Court judges has always been a highly visible political process, and the notion of 'constitutionalism' in American political thought lends some legitimacy to the judiciary's role of upholding the more enduring will of the people as expressed in the constitution over the will of any transient majority.[13]

Even so, American discussions of judicial power continue to display some uneasiness about treating the judiciary as a thoroughly political

11 Scott, 'Abolition of Appeals to the Privy Council – A Symposium,' (1947), 25 Can. Bar Rev. 566; Friedmann, 'Judges, Politics and the Law,' (1951), 29 Can. Bar Rev. 811; Laskin, 'Tests for the Validity of Legislation: What's the Matter?' (1955–6), 11 U.T.L.J. 114; MacGuigan, 'Precedent and Policy in the Supreme Court,' (1967), 45 Can. Bar Rev. 627; Weiler, 'Two Models of Judicial Decision-Making,' (1968), 46 Can. Bar Rev. 406, In the Last Resort (published in 1974 after this paper was prepared).
12 Russell, 'How Do Judges Decide? Ideology vs Science,' (April, 1972), Canadian Forum 6
13 See Alexander Hamilton's Federalist Paper No. 78. There is no counterpart to this in Canada's public political philosophy.

branch of government. There is a hankering, even among fairly thorough-going 'realists,' for a greater source of objectivity or rationality for judicial decisions than the attitudes or preferences of the judges.[14] When there is a reaction against the Supreme Court's interpretation of the constitution, there is a tendency for those who oppose the court's majority to accuse them of forgetting that it is not 'the business of courts to sit in judgment on the wisdom of legislative action'[15] or, to use the language of the Warren court's critics, to accuse the Supreme Court justices of not being 'strict constructionists.'

In Canada there has been as much, if not even more, concern to find a basis for objectivity, for removing judicial subjectivity from judicial decision-making even in areas where policy issues are admittedly unavoidable. Thus, the first generation of Canadian judicial realists were apt to talk rather glibly about judges adapting the constitution to the needs of the country or discovering a national or social consensus, much as one might find the law. A later generation of judicial realists has shown more scepticism of the judge's capacity for discovering some sociological natural law. Mark MacGuigan, for instance, after identifying the objectivity which he feels is inherent in the judicial process, concludes that 'this objectivity is unstable and incomplete, for the subjective element is inevitable, regardless of the jurisprudential theory invoked. We are thus in the last analysis compelled to accept even the subjectivity of judicial legislation, and seem to have only the choice of accepting it gratefully or grudgingly.'[16] Again, Paul Weiler, in prescribing an ideal model of judicial reasoning, admits that 'there is almost always an element of fiat within the narrow interstices left by the reasoning process.'[17]

It is certainly not difficult to think of important social issues brought for decision to our highest appellate courts for which objectively legally correct solutions cannot readily be ascertained. For instance, What degree of parental neglect justifies deviations from article 243 of Quebec's Civil Code which requires that a child remain under the authority of his parents until he comes of age?[18] Does Lord's Day observance legislation deny some Canadians the freedom of worship prescribed by the Canadian Bill of Rights?[19] Under our constitution can a province, after giving trade-unions the right to

---

14 See Wechsler *Principles, Politics, and Fundamental Law* (1961) and Bickel *The Least Dangerous Branch* (1962).
15 Mr Justice Stone's dissent in *U.S.* v *Butler*, (1935), 297 U.S. 1, at 87
16 Ibid, at 665
17 Weiler, supra note 11, at 431–2
18 *Taillon* v *Donaldson*, [1953] 2 S.C.R. 257
19 *Robertson and Rosetanni* v *The Queen*, [1963] S.C.R. 651

collect funds by a check-off prevent these unions from using the funds to support a political party?[20] In these and numerous other cases it is not easy, indeed it may be impossible, to work out answers which are clearly and incontestably 'in accord with the needs of society' or 'reflect the social consensus' or (least of all) are entailed by necessarily applicable legal doctrines.

There are some tendencies in the Canadian legal system which are apt to increase the occasions on which the courts, especially the senior appeal courts, are required to deviate from a narrow adjudicative role and consequently become more politically exposed. One such tendency is the reference case procedure – the long established practice in Canada, whereby the executive branch of government (federal or provincial) can require that the courts answer highly political, abstract, and hypothetical questions which are not at all 'ripe' for adjudication.[21] Two of the most recent instances, the *Offshore Mineral Rights* reference[22] and the *Chicken and Egg War* case,[23] plunged the Supreme Court into federal-provincial controversies. The court cannot be blamed for the decision of politicians to use the advisory opinion process as a stratagem in their political struggles. But the court, in responding to these reference questions, did not perform in a manner calculated to enhance its legitimacy.

In the *Offshore Mineral Rights* case the court, in finding a positive base for federal jurisdiction, employed the inherent national importance test in a most unconvincing way. With a simple, and somewhat arrogant, nationalist flourish the court asserted that 'the mineral resources of the lands underlying the territorial sea are of concern to Canada as a whole and go beyond local or provincial concern or interests.'[24] The political circumstances surrounding this case were already explosive enough without waving this particular red flag before the provinces. Several provinces had strenuously objected to referring this question to the court. Following the decision, the premier of Quebec, Mr Lesage, stated that 'if French-speaking Canadians' constitutional rights are to be protected, the Supreme Court of Canada – which rules on constitutional questions – must be either changed or replaced.'[25]

The *Chicken and Egg War* case required the court to give judgment in

20 *Oil, Chemical and Atomic Workers International Union* v *Imperial Oil*, [1963] s.c.r. 584
21 For a review of reference case procedure in Canada, see Strayer *Judicial Review of Legislation in Canada* (1968), ch 7.
22 *Reference Re: Offshore Mineral Rights*, [1967] s.c.r. 792
23 *A.-G. Man.* v *Manitoba Egg and Poultry Association*, [1971] s.c.r. 689
24 Ibid, at 817
25 *Globe and Mail*, 14 March 1967

the most feigned of cases. Manitoba, an egg-exporting province, in an attempt to combat a Quebec marketing scheme designed to secure a larger share of the provincial egg market for local producers, drafted legislation similar to Quebec's and asked the courts to rule on its validity. The Supreme Court obliged Manitoba by finding this faked piece of legislation invalid. It did so on the grounds that the legislation was aimed at restricting interprovincial trade and commerce, even though, as Mr Justice Laskin admitted, the essential factual data upon which such a finding must rest was not presented to the court.[26]

For the full implication of these decisions to be seen they should be placed in the context of the Supreme Court's over-all performance as our final constitutional umpire since 1949. During this period twenty-one provincial Acts have been found invalid (43 per cent of those challenged), whereas in not one of the twenty cases challenging federal Acts on constitutional grounds has the Supreme Court ruled against the federal level of government. While centralists may applaud the Supreme Court's strengthening of federal legislative power, they should consider the possibility that this very process may have weakened the judicial power of the Supreme Court. It is not accidental that the lengthiest section of the proposed charter for constitutional reform which emerged from the Victoria Conference in June 1971 concerned appointments to the Supreme Court of Canada. Increasing provincial demands to participate in the appointment of Supreme Court justices indicate a decline in the court's legitimacy as an acceptable umpire of our federal system. The politicization of the appointment process to the point where a judge may be viewed as a legislative representative of a particular sectional interest will surely reduce the Supreme Court's capacity to perform its role of constitutional arbitration in a judicious manner.

Another feature of our contemporary legal system which tends to accelerate the politicization of our courts is the Bill of Rights. My colleague, Donald Smiley, comments in his article in this collection on the dangers to the courts' legitimacy inherent in this expansion of judicial power into the area of fundamental rights and freedoms. The statutory Bill of Rights which we now have, even though it has no application to provincial governments, has already added significantly to the policy-making responsibilities of the courts.[27] A constitutional Bill of Rights will take this process much further. I am not concerned here with the wisdom of making such a change in our

26 Supra note 23, at 704
27 See especially *The Queen* v *Drybones*, [1970] s.c.r. 282.

system of government. What I wish to emphasize is the ironic way in which such a change might affect judicial power in Canada. The effect is likely to be ironic, for while increasing judicial power in one sense, this expansion of the court's power into sensitive areas of social policy may at the same time reduce judicial authority by eroding the popular image of our judiciary as the impartial arbiters of our legal disputes.

If the courts (especially the Supreme Court) are to assume the larger political role entailed by a constitutional Bill of Rights – and assume it successfully – several developments should occur. There will have to be wider public recognition of the Supreme Court as a *governing* branch of government, perhaps 'the least dangerous branch' – the official public philosopher charged with the task of reasoning through, as well as thoughtful mortals can, some of the major issues in our public ethics. To earn that recognition the courts, especially the nation's Supreme Court, will have to recruit to the bench judges with a considerably wider range of talents. To date, the quality of reasoning exhibited by the Supreme Court in its written judgments, with a few notable exceptions, has not been high. This is especially true in its first decisions on the meaning of the Canadian Bill of Rights.[28] An improvement in the calibre of jurists appointed to the highest courts of the nation and of the provinces may, among other things, require some modification of the monopoly that leaders of Canada's two major political parties, the Liberals and Conservatives, exercise over all appointments to senior courts in Canada. This monopoly means that outstanding lawyers associated with such important political movements as the NDP or anti-federalist parties in Quebec are virtually excluded from holding major judicial positions in Canada.

So far I have been guilty of what is perhaps the worst sin of political scientists who study the judiciary in focusing my discussion of judicial power almost exclusively on our highest appeal courts and their decisions on major issues of constitutional and public law. But these courts and these decisions are far from typical of judicial process in our society. At the trial level, and in our lower courts where nearly all of our judicial business is done, there may be little room for the kind of judicial lawmaking that goes on in appeal courts, if only because the decisions of these lower courts do not so readily become binding rules of law. But in the assessment of facts,

28 See, for instance, the majority's superficial treatment of the meaning of freedom of religion in *Robertson and Rosetanni*, supra note 19, and the majority's failure to explain clearly how its decision in the *Drybones* case is consistent with its interpretation of the Bill of Rights in *Robertson and Rosetanni*, or how its decision in *A.-G. Can.* v *Lavell* (1974) 38 D.L.R. (3d) 481 can be squared with the *Drybones* decision.

the determination of sentences, in procedural rulings, and in the application of general laws to particular circumstances there is plenty of leeway for the exercise of judicial discretion. In the exercise of this discretion, the attitudes of the judges, or, to use the term I would prefer, the thinking of the judges about social values, about the purpose of legal institutions, and about the credibility of different individuals may often be determining factors. The law, in fact, often does require that a judge exercise his judgment.

A growing awareness of this discretionary aspect of judging, coupled with a desire to confine the judiciary to the determination of matters which can be more tightly controlled by established legal rules, has led to some reduction in judicial power in many western societies, including our own. Legislatures have taken to codifying legal rules formerly determined by judge-made common law. Areas of adjudication have been taken away from the courts and assigned to other agencies or tribunals, where professional knowledge of a non-legal kind or more informal procedures are considered desirable. Currently, there is discussion in Canada, for instance, of removing the sentencing function of judges to a body of expert social scientists, and the application of our anti-monopoly and environment protection legislation to experts in economics, commerce, or engineering.[29]

Judicial power may be threatened in another way, a deeper way, which is far more worrisome. That is, there may be some reduction in the authority of courts, some diminution of the respect they command from the public they serve. This is particularly likely during a period when radical or minority political groups are apt to use court trials as vehicles for advancing their political cause. Such an erosion of the judiciary's political authority could be particularly serious in those areas of adjudication where courts continue, and in an orderly society must continue, to function.

Here we need some historical perspective. Those who may now decry the partisan quality of Canadian justice should not forget that the Canadian judicial system in little more than a century has gone through a tremendous process of development from the crude, harsh, version of backwoods, frontier justice which prevailed in this part of North America in the late eighteenth and early nineteenth centuries. I invite any reader who doubts this to examine Hilda Neatby's classic study, *Justice Under the Quebec Act*,[30] which reveals that the judicial system was not only the hottest

29 See Hogarth *Sentencing as a Human Process* (1971) and Donald Dewees's article in this volume.
30 Neatby *The Administration of Justice under the Quebec Act* (1937)

political issue but also the most partisan branch of government in the earliest days of British North America. She gives us this description of the colony's Court of Appeal in the 1780s (a court constituted by the executive council of the colony):

A little legal learning and experience would have been useful to this court, for its task was not easy ... Not only was there no attempt to acquire a detailed knowledge of the laws; there was not even an effort to reach an agreement upon the general system of law which ought to prevail. After the records of a case had been examined and the opposing lawyers heard, it was usual for each member of the court to give his vote, beginning with the most junior and proceeding to the president. The ultimate decision was often determined not by the justice of the cause, or the eloquence of the lawyers, but by the prevailing racial flavour of the court.[31]

Similarly, Dale and Lee Gibson's recent volume tracing the evolution of legal institutions in Manitoba reminds us of the precarious and rough-hewn nature of Manitoba justice in the long period of company rule up to 1870.[32] These early departures from judicial virtues were not simply aberrations of the wild west or the British conquest of New France; the early history of Upper Canada also has many a tale of unruly, unlearned, and unsavoury judges.[33]

In the late nineteenth and twentieth centuries, two major changes have occurred in the character of Canadian courts. First, a moderate separation of powers,[34] reinforced by security of judicial tenure, has given the judiciary reasonable insulation from direct interference by other branches of government. Secondly, the Canadian judiciary has been profession-alized. The process of professionalization advanced unevenly across the country, displaying the usual metropolitan bias in the growth of judicial systems.[35] But the professional bench has by now become the norm in all

31 Ibid, at 136
32 Gibson and Gibson *Substantial Justice: Law and Lawyers in Manitoba 1670–1970* (1972)
33 See, for instance, Kennedy's account of Justice Robert Thorpe in *The Constitution of Canada 1534–1937* (1938), 122–6.
34 The separation of powers in Canada is moderate, in that a prime residue of judicial power is not explicitly guaranteed in the written constitution, although it may be implicitly guaranteed for the provincial courts under ss 96 and 99 of the BNA Act. See Lederman, 'The Independence of the Judiciary,' (1956), 34 *Can. Bar Rev.* 769.
35 Professional lawyers, particularly those of some distinction, are primarily metropolitan creatures, so that the hinterland is the last to receive the alleged advantages of their presiding over the judicial process. Not only does this help to explain the extended use of lay magistrates in rural areas but it also had something to do with the relative difficulty in recruiting outstanding lawyers from Montreal or Toronto to the Canadian Supreme Court in Ottawa. See Biggar, 'The Selection of Judges,' (1933), 11 *Can. Bar Rev.* 27.

parts of Canada and threatens to eliminate the last important vestige of popular participation in the administration of justice – the jury trial.

These developments in our judicial system went hand-in-hand with the cultivation of the notion that judging is the entirely technical task of objectively identifying the correct legal solution to judicial disputes. Indeed, as I have suggested, in a democratic age, the independence of the judiciary from popular control could most easily be justified by insisting that judging was purely technical and denying that the judiciary had any real power. But this image of a powerless, entirely technical, or mechanical judiciary has in recent years been wearing rather thin. This is partly because of the growing awareness of the discretionary power which has always and necessarily been exercised by judges. It may also reflect the demand of a more egalitarian and welfare-oriented society for an improved quality of judicial service.

If an independent judiciary is to survive as an effective branch of government in Canada, there will have to be a better understanding of the necessary bias of such an institution. We shall have to find a more convincing way of making judicial power legitimate than denying its existence. Harold Innis, amongst others, taught us that every institution has its bias.[36] In this sense, no institution, including courts, can be absolutely impartial. The necessary and most fundamental bias of an independent judiciary in our society is perhaps best understood by recognizing the bias of courts in more optimistic or revolutionary societies such as the Soviet Union.

There, the primary bias or aim of the judicial process, as I understand it, is to contribute to the Marxist-Leninist education and remolding of the citizen, so that ultimately no courts will be necessary. Nikolai Nikolaievich, a Moscow judge, in an interview with the American author George Feifer gives this explanation of the purpose of Soviet courts:

The point is that we are reconstructing men's consciousness already ... through the work of the courts, for one thing. First of all, every single violation must be uncovered and punished. With no exceptions. Everyone must know for certain that it is futile to break the law ... Law enforcement must *expand* before it withers away. FEIFER: Some philosophers say that crime is part of human nature, inherent in the human condition. NIKOLAIEVICH: Nonsense, I must say. There is no such thing as human nature. Man is the product of his surroundings, of the social and economic system which molds him. Change the mold and you change the man. And that is what we are doing ...

36 Innis *The Bias of Communication* (1951)

Don't damn us because we haven't yet succeeded. We know that. But you aren't even trying. You laugh at our goals and let yourselves slide deeper into crime in the name of a theory of man – and then call *us* dogmatic.[37]

Nikolai is right. We are dogmatic. A belief in original sin is built into our judicial institutions. We are a more sceptical people, and our best, or at least our deeper, instincts tell us that there will always be disputes about the correct application of the binding rules of our society, including constitutional rules defining the powers of our governors. Hence the continuing need for judicial institutions staffed by knowledgeable persons with a capacity for fairness and reasonableness and not controlled in the substance of their decision-making by other branches of government. Hence, the continuing need in our society for the performance of the judicial task of sorting out for case-by-case application the various considerations and (often conflicting) norms which constitute that portion of our ethical system we have chosen to enforce.

But, while we should come to acknowledge and understand the necessary bias of our judicial institutions, it is equally important to eliminate from their operation any unnecessary biases which prevent them from performing the act of judging well for all citizens. This is not the place for a full-scale discussion of judicial reform. But two biases of our existing system require some comment.

The first is the degree to which the class system and materialistic values associated with our version of capitalism mar our judicial system. Many illustrations could be given, but one feature which stands out is the failure to provide the best judges and decent facilities for our basic criminal courts where the vast majority of Canadians who are brought to trial experience Canadian justice.[38] If most of those being tried were affluent members of the middle or upper middle class, I doubt that these lower court facilities would have remained so inadequate for so long. This surely reflects the unwillingness of our political elites to direct public expenditure to social goods primarily of concern to the poorer people in our society. Or, to take another example, our practice of basing the right of appeal on the amount of money involved in a dispute means that an individual or corporation disputing any claim in excess of $10,000 has a right to appeal to the Supreme Court of Canada, a right which may be denied to a person sentenced to life imprisonment.[39] This entails a reprehensibly materialistic

37 Feifer *Justice in Moscow* (1964), at 330–1
38 See Friedland, 'Magistrates Courts: Functioning and Facilities,' (1968), 11 *Crim. L.Q.* 52.
39 R.S.C. 1970, C.S-19, S 36(a)

way of measuring the importance of civil rights and rationing access to our highest court.[40]

The second bias concerns a tradition of amateurism in judicial administration. Judicial administration in the English-speaking world has been the last stronghold of the upper-class amateur in government, muddling through. Canada has lagged behind both the United States and Great Britain in even the basic matter of obtaining accurate and useful statistical information on the work of courts.[41] There are now some real signs of progress on this front in a number of Canadian jurisdictions.[42] These efforts are to be applauded, for the principle of judicial independence should not be permitted to insulate the judiciary from the requirement of fairly and effectively distributing judicial services. In Canada, reform of judicial administration has an additional obstacle to overcome in that the constitutional division of powers leaves the federal government with the responsibility of appointing and paying the judges of major provincial courts, the provincial government with the responsibility for establishing these courts, and no level of government with an over-all responsibility for the provision of an efficient judicial service.

But I suspect that the most serious obstacle to a more effective provision of judicial services may be that, for too many lawyers and judges, judging is still not regarded as the provision of a basic social service but the exercise of a private professional craft.

PETER RUSSELL is a professor of political science and principal of Innis College, University of Toronto. A former Rhodes scholar from the University of Toronto, he has concentrated his scholarly activities on the judicial process and has written a number of books and studies, including *The Supreme Court of Canada as a Bilingual and Bicultural Institution* (1969), and edited *Nationalism in Canada* (1966). He is at present completing a book entitled *The Judicial Process in Canada*.

40 Since writing the above, the *Report of the Special Committee of the Canadian Bar Association on the Caseload of the Supreme Court of Canada* (1973) has been published which recommends (pp 8–9) the 'abolition of appeals as of right in civil cases to the Supreme Court of Canada.' In October, 1974 a Bill was introduced in the Senate to accomplish this.
41 My own first exposure to this phenomenon was in carrying out a study of the Supreme Court of Canada for the Royal Commission on Bilingualism and Biculturalism, when I discovered that no statistical record of the court's work had been maintained.
42 For example, the research project of Robert Hann of the Centre of Criminology, University of Toronto, *Decision-Making in the Canadian Criminal Court System: A Systems Analysis* (1973), *The MacKimmie Report* (1973), on the judicial system of Prince Edward Island, and the Ontario Law Reform Commission's *Report on Administration of Ontario Courts* (1973).

DONALD SMILEY

Courts, legislatures, and the protection of human rights

This paper examines in a Canadian context the appropriateness of judicial as against legislative decision in the definition and ranking of human rights. The issue is often put within the framework of proposals for the further entrenchment of human rights in the Canadian constitution. In support of such proposals, as they were made a couple of decades ago, it was often asserted that such entrenchment was necessary for Canada to discharge its international obligations. The isolationism of current Canadian attitudes and policies makes this kind of argument less common now.

As Ronald Cheffins has pointed out in private conversation, the term 'entrenchment' has no accepted meaning in Canadian constitutional law or practice. I here take it to mean one or more constitutional amendments which would place the human rights so designated in those parts of the constitution most difficult of subsequent amendment. Barring a new amending procedure, this would mean that these rights could be redefined in the future only by the United Kingdom Parliament so enacting in response to a joint address by the Senate and House of Commons of Canada. By constitutional convention, but by convention only, such action by the Canadian Parliament would take place only after the consent of all the provinces had been secured. If there were entrenchment, some provisions could be so explicitly embodied in the constitution as to preclude any subsequent doubt or need for interpretation about their meaning. Such provisions might include, for example, a prohibition against any Canadian being deprived of his citizenship or a prescription stating that the life of Parliament or a provincial legislature should not extend beyond five years.

Most provisions related to human rights, however, would necessarily be expressed in general language conferring on the courts of law the responsibility of defining and ranking rights in an ongoing process of judicial review of the constitution.

The issue of judicial as against legislative definition of human rights remains whether or not there is further entrenchment. *Drybones*[1] appears to have established the 1960 Bill of Rights[2] as a constitutional statute in the sense that federal legislation deemed by the courts to be contrary to its provisions is invalid, whether such legislation was enacted before or after 1960 but excepting those circumstances where Parliament and/or the federal cabinet was acting under the authority of the War Measures Act or when Parliament explicitly enacted that specific legislation was to be operative notwithstanding the Bill of Rights. (It is possible too that activist courts might come to find in the human rights legislation of some or all of the provinces similar prohibitions against provincial law contravening these provisions.)[3] However, it must be remembered that *Drybones* posed clear alternatives to the Supreme Court of Canada because the terms of 94(*b*) of the Indian Act[4] were unambiguously contrary to the provisions of the 1960 Bill of Rights enjoining racial discrimination. Future challenges to federal legislation are unlikely to present the Supreme Court of Canada with such open-and-shut choices as did *Drybones*, and so the actual role of the judiciary in the definition of human rights is in doubt. The most radical proposal for an active role for the courts in this connection has been made by J. Noel Lyon and Ronald G. Atkey in their recent textbook on Canadian constitutional law.[5] The authors are impatient of what they call the 'division of powers approach' of judicial interpretation of the Canadian constitution in respect to human rights, that is, the approach which denies that rights have any independent constitutional value and proceeds on the basis that the sole function of judicial review is to delineate the respective

---

1 *The Queen* v *Drybones* [1970] S.C.R. 282; cf. *A.-G.* v *Lavell* (1974) 38 D.L.R. (3d) 481 (S.C.C.)
2 Canadian Bill of Rights, R.S.C. 1970, app. III
3 The first provincial bill of rights was enacted by Saskatchewan. Interestingly, the incumbent federal minister of justice, the Honourable Otto Lang, challenged the constitutional validity of this enactment in 1959 while he was a member of the College of Law of the University of Saskatchewan on the general grounds that the bill trespassed on Parliament's powers over the criminal law and criminal procedure: (1959) 37 *Can. Bar Rev.* 233.
4 Now R.S.C. 1970, c. I-6, s. 95
5 *Canadian Constitutional Law in a Modern Perspective* (1970), particularly part 4. For my critical review of this treatment of human rights see (1972) 50 *Can. Bar Rev.* 139.

legislative jurisdictions of Parliament and the provinces. Here is the counterprescription of Lyon and Atkey: 'If a fundamental rights issue is clearly perceived, a court should attempt to meet the issue head-on, and should be loath to allow *any* level of government to deny this right through claims that it is merely acting within its proper sphere of legislative jurisdiction.'[6] This advice to the courts is not tied explicitly to any prior constitutional entrenchment of human rights.

Rights are claims for specified kinds of treatment made by or on behalf of particular individuals or groups. When we speak of rights it is always necessary to be clear whether we are speaking in the indicative or imperative moods. For example, what is the meaning of this statement: 'Irrespective of my financial circumstances, I have the right to medical and hospital care at public expense when I need these services'? It would depend on the context. If the statement was made by a Canadian he would be doing nothing else than describing the circumstances provided for by the province of which he was a legal resident. But an American making this statement would be saying something quite different – that although health services are not available to all at public expense they *should* be. Thus, despite the indicative form of the Declaration of Independence, men do not have the rights to 'life, liberty and the pursuit of happiness' in the same way as they have eyes and legs and livers. It may be, although I do not want to pursue this point further, that our confusions on this matter spring from the tradition of natural law, with its failure to distinguish adequately between law as empirical generalization, law as ethical imperative, and law as the authoritative command of political superior.

How then do we distinguish human rights from other human claims? And, when rights conflict, what principles do we use in ranking them? This was less of a problem in societies more traditional and more cohesive than our own. What we used to call 'primitive man' accepted the structures of power and privilege in his tribe as givens, like the physical environment: in Karl Popper's terms he did not distinguish between the laws of nature and normative laws. And as students of the law will understand better than I do, our own constitutional traditions have their roots in a time when monarchs and courts and parliament 'found' the law in the settled traditions of the community. How different it is today when new claims made in the name of 'rights' are being demanded every year and demanded in terms of what purport to be transcendental principles. We can perhaps sympathize with de Tocqueville when he said, referring to the predisposition of his French

6 Ibid, at 377; emphasis in text

compatriots for general political ideas, 'I am informed, every morning when I wake that some general and eternal law has just been discovered, which I never heard mentioned before. There is not a mediocre scribbler who does not try his hand at discovering truths applicable to a great kingdom, and who is very ill pleased with himself if he does not succeed in compressing the human race into the compass of an article.'[7]

At the risk of seeming pedantic, I am going to outline a few areas where in the near future new developments in the definition and ranking of human rights may be upon us.

First, we may experience difficulties in reconciling egalitarian rights with certain emergent demands of pluralism. The 1960 Bill of Rights enjoins discrimination on the basis of 'race, national origin, colour, religion or sex.' The thrust here is that these are invalid legal categories determining the treatment of people under the provisions of federal law or executive action. But let us say that previously disadvantaged groups decide they cannot attain equality on these terms. For example, women might come to conclude that formal political equality was not enough and demand that females be assured control of a set of political institutions, or at least guaranteed parity with men with respect to these institutions. In the United States many blacks have put aside their former pressures for integration and a 'color-blind constitution' in favour of black power. Perhaps some of the most crucial clashes between egalitarianism and pluralism may come in education. It has been asserted that in its approach to public education the Warren court in the United States was both integrationist and assimilationist. But today some of the most enlightened reformers are pressing for diversification and experimentation in education and the fragmentation of our somewhat monolithic state and provincial systems.

Second, we are obviously in a period of rapid redefinition of economic rights. A couple of generations ago these were of course defined almost entirely in terms of the ownership of property. More recently, the most crucial of economic rights have come to be associated with employment – the right to join trade unions, collective bargaining, contributory retirement pensions financed partly from employers' contributions, workmen's compensation, industrial standards, minimum wages, and so on. These rights developed in a period when governments became committed more explicitly than ever before to maintaining full employment and full employment meant enhancing the total material productivity of the community. Perhaps such conditions are changing, and in an economy characterized by

7 2 *Democracy in America* (1954, Vintage Books, New York), at 15

capital-intensive industry and relatively high minimum wages we may find that we can enhance our material prosperity by employing only a portion of the available work force. Surely this would involve significant changes in our definition of economic rights.

Third, we are in the process of redefining rights with respect to sexual activity. Among those who regard themselves as enlightened there are pressures to remove legal restrictions on such activities between – and among – consenting adults, although not even on the University of Toronto campus has there come into existence a group proclaiming the liberating nature of adult incest. Apart from the adults, a recent television programme informs me that even the smallest children have sexual urges and thus, in the arguments of some students of the subject, sexual rights, and we shall no doubt soon have a demand that these rights be entrenched in a new Canadian constitution. But my serious concern is the redefinition of sexual rights in what one might call a regime of reliable contraception under which, unless there is compelling evidence to the contrary, the 'reasonable man' can assume that conception has resulted from a deliberate act of a man and a woman. Such a circumstance surely redefines in a radical way the relation between sexual activity and procreation and will, I think, make it difficult to maintain the latter as a purely private matter in the face of the pressures of the public authorities to influence the size and genetic quality of their populations.

Fourth and lastly, there are challenges in the confinement and compulsory treatment of deviants. Merton A. Kaplan has asked, 'As anti-social behavior becomes less tolerable as a result of the increasing complexity and crowding of society, are we not likely to treat what we cannot tolerate?'[8] We are aware of how such methods are being used in the Soviet Union to deal with political dissenters. I am not sure our own society deserves self-congratulation. Under circumstances where we have come to define even the most extreme cases of deviation in terms of illness rather than crime and where we place a high value on social adjustment there are clear and present dangers in our new-found techniques of compulsory rehabilitation, particularly, perhaps, in group psychotherapy.

When we come to look at human rights in any specific way we see that they are conditioned by time, place, and circumstance. For example, the United Nations Declaration of Human Rights of only a quarter-century ago has nothing to say about the rights to public information, to an environment

8 'A Nightmare,' Weinstein ed, *The Political Experience: Readings in Political Science* (1972), at 376

free of pollution, or to public services in one's own language in multilingual communities. Despite the circumstantial nature of rights, much contemporary discussion proceeds with a regrettable lack of humility. We are inclined to believe that the rights we now protect demonstrate that we are more enlightened than our predecessors. But because we are so entranced by our own circumstances and commitments, we seek, through constitutional entrenchment, to fasten our solutions on the future or, more accurately, to make it very difficult for these solutions to be overturned by those who come after us. There *were* provisions entrenching certain human rights in the British North America Act of 1867 – provisions related to the educational rights of denominational minorities and to areas in Quebec where anglophones were then dominant in numbers. Many of us would argue that such entrenched rights are today an unfortunate inheritance. Contrary to the spirit and practice of entrenchment there is profound wisdom in the master-tradition of the British parliamentary system which affirms that, with one exception, a legislature can enact as it chooses, either as sovereign or within the limits imposed by a constitutional division of legislative powers. That single – and crucial – exception is that it cannot bind future parliaments.

Most discussions of legislative as against judicial decision with respect to human rights proceed according to conflicting views of what I call democratic fundamentalism.

The first view asserts that in terms of democratic theory elected officials have better claims than courts to define and rank human rights as well as to make other important decisions about public policy. Democracy in this view is government in accord with the will of the governed, and the organs of government best able and most likely to act in accord with this will are composed of people who have successfully contested popular elections – and act in anticipation of future elections. I do not find this argument completely convincing. If we look at the operative constitution of any developed political system – the constitution in action as against the constitution of the textbooks of law or civics – we find a complex allocation of discretionary powers. Powers are wielded in various kinds of matters by judges and juries, by political executives and career bureaucrats, by elected legislatures and political parties, by the electorate, by the groups who effect constitutional amendment. And we also find different kinds of procedural rules for reaching various kinds of decisions – unanimous consent in jury verdicts, certain motions in the House of Commons and the most crucial of constitutional amendments, consensual decision-making at federal-provincial conferences and, perhaps, in cabinets, pluralities, bare majorities and extraordinary majorities as so defined, different provisions for quorums, and so on. On this basis, I would see no a priori reason stemming from democratic theory which would prevent a democratic community from conferring decisions involving human rights on the courts or from enacting provisions respecting such rights other than those which prevail in respect to ordinary lawmaking.

The contrary view of democratic fundamentalism asserts that the majoritarian processes of public decision can and should operate after what are regarded as fundamental human rights are, so to speak, fenced off from the action of these processes. As Peter Russell has argued, the claim that elected politicians in Canada or other western democracies usually act in response to mobilized public majorities contradicts all we know about the operations of this kind of government.[9] On all but infrequent occasions such majorities are not mobilized in matters of human rights or public policy. But even if this version of democracy is accepted, there is the problem of defining what the secured rights should be. The document, *A Canadian Charter of Human Rights*, introduced by Mr Trudeau as minister of justice into the first Federal-Provincial Constitutional Conference proposes entrenchment of rights categorized as political, legal, egalitarian, and linguistic.[10] The Report of the Ontario Royal Commission of Inquiry into Civil Rights points out that the White Paper does not give any reason for including these claims or failing to include others.[11] The McRuer commission itself made a dichotomous classification of human rights which is to me more defensible. This classification suggested that the individual citizen should be recognized to have two basic categories of rights, A/ the right to participation in the process by which the basic circumstances under which the community is governed are decided, including its definition and ranking of human rights, B/ the right to be dealt with by the public authorities according to fair and impartial procedures. The McRuer Report formulated this classification in its sophisticated and persuasive argument *against* the entrenchment of rights. But even if these categories were used to sustain the opposite case, they give only the most general guidance about which claims are to be recognized as fundamental and which are not. Support for this second version of democratic fundamentalism is most characteristic of those who support one variant or other of the tradition of natural law, and R.H.S. Crossman has recently asserted that the British

9 'A Democratic Approach to Civil Liberties,' (1969) 19 *U.T.L.J.* 109, reprinted in Vaughan, Kyba, and Dwivedi eds, *Contemporary Issues in Canadian Politics* (1970), at 83
10 (1968)
11 (1969), Report No. 2, vol. 4, at 1529

have retained parliamentary supremacy as the fundamental principle of their constitution because they do not believe in natural law.[12] It seems to me, however, that the connection between the preferred procedures for protecting human rights and natural law is historical and psychological rather than logical in the sense that if the imperatives of natural law are binding surely they bind legislatures as much as courts. Which of the two sets of institutions will better protect such rights is thus a matter of prudential political judgment rather than political philosophy. To such judgment I now turn.

One of the first questions that arises is whether legislatures or courts are most accessible to those where rights are most in need of definition and protection: the deprived and the unpopular. This is a matter of time, place, and circumstance, but on the whole I think the advantage rests with legislatures. There are, of course, conditions under which those who have little access to or influence with elected politicians do get effective remedies from the courts, as was the case with Joseph Drybones[13] and a decade and more ago with the Jehovah's Witnesses in Quebec, who had the remarkable legal talents of Glen How and Frank Scott to act on their behalf. But under the more usual circumstances the deprived and the unpopular do not have such resources, either through emergent schemes of public legal aid or through private agencies commanding a reservoir of specialized legal skills. Even more crucially, Canadian law provides as yet a relatively narrow definition of legal standing, of the conditions under which individuals or groups are regarded as having a sufficiently direct interest in legislation to qualify as litigants pressing judicial challenges to its validity.[14]

I turn for a moment to the efficacy of bills of rights as instruments of public education. This kind of argument has an immediate appeal; all of us would agree that in the long run, if not the short, the effective protection of human rights must rest on widespread public tolerance and respect for these rights. From this perspective, a great deal has been claimed for the educative value of an entrenched charter of human rights, and in even broader terms the Canadian constitution has been subjected to much recent

12 *Inside View: Three Lectures on Prime Ministerial Government* (1972), at 113
13 For a journalist's account of the circumstances of *Drybones* see Corelli, 'How an Indian Changed Canada's Civil Rights Laws – The Drybones Case,' *Toronto Daily Star* 2 Jan. 1970, reprinted in Fox ed, *Politics: Canada* (3d ed, 1970) 495
14 There seems to have been little debate on judicial standing in Canada and almost no analysis of this crucial matter by enthusiasts for judicial activism in the protection of human rights. For a discussion of the existing Canadian law relating to standing in constitutional cases, see Strayer *Judicial Review of Legislation in Canada* (1968), at 96–125.

criticism because it does not, in any way meaningful to most citizens, state the fundamental purposes of the Canadian community. I confess to limited expectations for a creedal constitution as a vehicle of political education, and it is interesting to note that the Christian churches, which have had considerable experience in these matters, are now little disposed toward elaborate creedal affirmations in sustaining a living faith. Almost inevitably, a charter of human rights will promise more than it can deliver and by proclaiming that rights are absolute will attempt to disguise that they are not. From the point of view of the community as a whole, the entrenchment of human rights by its very nature removes from the control of elected representatives the power to make decisions about important public matters and thus in my view contributes to political immaturity. But in another sense are judges appropriate educators in the ideals of the polity? A former teacher of mine, Charles Hyneman, in his analysis of the Supreme Court of the United States argues that they are not.[15] According to his argument, the characteristic activity of a court of law ends in the coercive act, the decision, enforced if need be by the monopoly of physical force at the command of government. Hyneman asserts that there is wisdom in conferring the task of enunciating the highest ideals of society on those who do not have such coercive power – in my terms, though not his, on priests and poets and professors and playwrights. Thus he concludes 'There is a place for persuasion and there is a place for force in the progress of a people to higher ethical levels. The judicial office was constructed for the coercive act, not for argument, pleading, exhortation. The traffic of judges in ethical standards must be confined to standards that can be made effective in conduct by orders for compliance.'[16]

I want to discuss for a few moments what the McRuer Report calls 'sophistication' in the definition and ranking of human rights. The report says 'The fact is that the well-drafted statute passed in a democratic parliament under the cabinet system with full debate and under scrutiny of freely expressed public opinion is the most flexible and sophisticated form of law-making available under a constitutional system that puts human individual rights first.'[17] In summary form, the following are some of the elements of sophistication in which legislatures appear to have advantages over courts.

First, the legislature is in control of its own agenda. With respect to human rights and other matters of public policy it can deal with the matters

15 *The Supreme Court on Trial* (1963), at 270–5
16 Ibid, at 274
17 McRuer, supra note 11, at 1592–3

it wishes and can change completely or modify its previous decisions as circumstances warrant. The Canadian courts, on the other hand, deal with matters brought before them by others, whether as the result of litigation or as demands for advisory opinions by federal or provincial governments.

Second, the government has wide discretion in the forms by which it expresses its will. It may legislate in great detail, or it may outline only broad purposes while delegating more specific definitions to executive agencies, quasi-public or private associations, and courts. Courts for the most part are precluded in judicial review from devising complex solutions to complex problems. Apart from advisory opinions, they deal directly only with the specific issues raised by the conflict between particular litigants and in passing on the validity of legislation say only Yes or No. Further, in the Anglo-Canadian tradition, the decisions of courts are addressed to bar and bench rather than the wider public; both majority and minority opinions in *Drybones*, for example, were expressed in a form unintelligible to the average concerned citizen.

Third, the legislature has very wide powers to enforce its will. It can create enforcement agencies of the nature it believes appropriate, confer funds on these agencies, and bring their officials to account. The courts of law have relatively limited powers to ensure that its decisions are carried out. In circumstances involving human rights a more active role assumed by the judiciary will inevitably bring the courts into conflict with elected bodies, and in these situations the courts have limited powers of enforcement.

Fourth, in coming to decision the legislature has the power to take into account any considerations it wishes – public and expert opinion, cost to the public treasury, administrative feasibility, and so on – and has full discretion to weigh conflicting considerations as it believes appropriate. The courts on the other hand are precluded from taking into explicit account more than a narrow range of circumstances, limited by the main thrust of the Anglo-Canadian tradition to the dictionary meaning of the words contained in the constitution and other enactments and to precedents in cases deemed to be similar. There are of course strong currents of argument suggesting that Canadian courts, in reviewing the constitution at least, should take judicial notice of a broader range of matters than is usually done – for example, the opinion of experts on social and economic matters and the expressed purposes of legislators in respect to enactments being subjected to judicial challenge. On the other hand, even the most enthusiastic of judicial activists will wish to draw the line somewhere, and none of them so far as I know has suggested that in human rights cases the courts should inquire into the levels of public acceptance of such rights.

There remains the question of judicial legitimacy, in this context the continuing authority that Canadians by their attitudes and actions confer on the courts of law. Canadians appear to be a relatively deferential people in the face of the organs of public authority. Nowhere is this deference more fully manifested than in public attitudes toward the courts. One may recall the opprobrium to which David Lewis was subjected by the media and his political opponents when, in the context of the strike in the Quebec public service in April 1972, the NDP leader impugned the impartiality of the judiciary in such matters. Judicial moonlighting in the recent past became something of a minor scandal in Ontario,[18] and governments in Canada, presumably in harmony with prevailing opinion, continue to appoint judges as members of royal commissions, labour tribunals, and agencies to redraw the boundaries of electoral constituencies, and so on.[19] If judges assume a more aggressive role in the definition and ranking of human rights they will inevitably be more prominent in the popular consciousness and more subject to public criticism than before. And when they do get into the political arena, on what reservoirs of public legitimacy will they draw? In the United States the constitution has for nearly two centuries assumed a central and symbolic role in the structure of political allegiance. The courts – and in particular of course the Supreme Court of the United States – derive their legitimacy as the authoritative interpreter of the constitution, although there is a continuing tradition of this legitimacy being challenged. The British North America Act is not now and has never been the symbolic focus of Canadian nationhood, although until perhaps a decade ago Canadians were taught a decent respect for it as the legal foundation of their political community. Recent years have seen a massive denigration of the Canadian constitution[20] – by Quebec nationalists, by those who asserted that because the constitution was a century old it was ipso facto obsolete, by federal and provincial officials who found constitutional review a diversion from more useful and urgent public concerns. Unfortunately this attack on the constitution was made in its most extreme form by Lyon and

18 'Extra-Judicial Employment of Judicial Personnel,' *McRuer Report*, Report No. 1, vol. 2, part II, section 3. Ontario has taken action to decrease such employment.

19 The Electoral Boundaries Readjustment Act of 1964, now R.S.C. 1970, c. E-2, by which federal constituencies are reapportioned after each decennial census, provides that this be done by an Electoral Boundaries Commission for each province, the chairman being appointed by the chief justice of each province from 'among the judges of the court over which he presides.' T.H. Qualter remarks: 'The insistence on involving a judge in the redistribution procedure is peculiarly Canadian and it seems rather difficult to understand the rationale for it.' *The Election Process in Canada* (1970), at 101.

20 Cairns, 'The Living Canadian Constitution,' (1970), 77 *Queen's Quarterly* 1

Atkey, who assert that unless Canada can break away from the 'English constitution,' and in particular from the central tradition of legislative supremacy, our country 'would have been better advised to remain a colony.'[21] As we have seen, these writers prescribe a much more active role for the courts while at the same time disparaging the constitutional foundations of the Canadian political community.

Perhaps some will agree with most of this but still maintain that, on balance, courts will be wiser and more zealous than elected bodies in defining and ranking human rights. In much of the argument for entrenchment there is the underlying premise that the community needs to be saved from the inherently illiberal tendencies of public opinion because these create irresistible pressures on elected legislatures. Perhaps. It is my own impression, however, that in Canada the elected political elites are considerably more liberal than are the prevailing sentiments in their respective local, provincial, and national electorates. Again, it is my impression that when we begin to inquire carefully into those institutions of Canadian society under the direct control of the bar and the bench we will find less than a total commitment to humane values. There is a strain of absolutism in recent Canadian proposals for an entrenched Bill of Rights. Prime Minister Trudeau said in 1969, 'To enshrine a right in a constitutional charter is to make an important judgment, to give to that right of the individual a higher order of value than the right of government to infringe it.'[22] This argument proceeds on the assumption that encroachments on human rights are always unequivocal and disinterested and liberal people will always be able to agree when such encroachments are made. Again, if we take Mr Trudeau's statement literally, there is the assumption that under all conceivable circumstances entrenched rights are to prevail over other considerations. These absolutist premises are in practice indefensible. In the sphere of human rights there is indeed an economy, and rights have what economists call 'opportunity costs,' in the sense that to get something of value it is necessary to give up something else of value.

As a non-lawyer, it seems clear to me that if Canadian courts are to assume a more active role in the ranking and defining of human rights there must be profound changes in the Canadian legal culture. Canadian jurists are profoundly in the positivist tradition. But the determination of human rights in particular circumstances is in Peter Russell's terms the 'delicate balancing of social priorities.'[23] I confess not to know the shape of the new jurisprudence or how judges and legal scholars are going to get us to realize

21 Lyon and Atkey, supra note 5, at v
22 *The Constitution and the People of Canada* (1969), at 20

it while maintaining the continuity with past traditions and lines of judicial interpretation that is surely necessary in our kind of polity. I confess also that the break proposed by Atkey and Lyon is too radical for me. But perhaps there should be a warning to enthusiasts for a socially relevant jurisprudence. This approach by its nature downgrades the technical nature of the law, and when members of bar and bench set up shop to articulate the political needs and political ideals of the community they enter a world in which others make the same claims. To be blunt: as piety does not make a theologian or pugnacity a military strategist, an increasing social sensitivity among lawyers and judges is no substitute for intellectual discipline in the social sciences and political philosophy.

To return to the main argument of this paper, I quote what I said on a previous occasion:

Apart from those times where public opinion is inflamed, the democratic legislature is uniquely equipped to make sound judgements about human rights. In my view Parliament has been at or near its best in some of the debates about human rights in the past decade – debates in respect to capital punishment, divorce, abortion, hate literature, official languages. Although the determination of the scope and nature of human rights usually involves some technical considerations, the technical content of reasoned discussion and decision is characteristically not as high as in regard to, say, defence policy or environmental pollution. Thus the major considerations in respect to human rights ordinarily involve the clash of human values, the sense of the community about what is acceptable and the broadest judgements of where society is going. Further, questions involving human rights tend not to be as localized in their incidence as is true of many other public policies and the Member of Parliament may well be more free to act primarily as a member of a deliberative body rather than a voice of particularized constituency interests. Elected politicians working within an environment of public discussion and debate are well equipped to deal wisely with questions of human rights. It is yet to be demonstrated that the Canadian judiciary can do better.[24]

DONALD SMILEY, a graduate of the University of Alberta and Northwestern University, is a professor of political science, University of Toronto, having taught at the University of British Columbia. A former president of the Canadian Political Science Association, he has written several books, including *The Canadian Political Nationality* (1967) and *Canada in Question: Federalism in the Seventies* (1972). He is now the editor of *Canadian Public Administration*.

23 Russell, supra note 9, at 123
24 25 *Minutes of Proceedings and Evidence of the Special Joint Committee of the Senate and of the House of Commons on the Constitution of Canada* (17 Dec. 1970), at 43

JAMES GIFFEN

The criminal courts and the control of addictions

A paper concerned mainly with public policy in dealing with Skid Row alcoholics and opiate addicts may appear to bear a tenuous relationship to courts and trials. However, the choice of topic can be justified on the ground that the forms of social control employed in the attempt to deal with behaviour defined as undesirable by those who influence public policy can greatly affect the operation of the courts. A heavy reliance on the criminal justice system in preference to other modes of control or to official non-intervention can put a heavy load on the courts. This, in turn, may create pressures to develop informal practices that expedite trials at the expense of the ideals of the adversary system or cause hardships and criticism of the law's delays. Where the courts are forced to bring the awesome power of the state to bear on behaviour which is widely felt to be inappropriate for criminal sanctioning, the system loses some of the respect that is a condition of its successful functioning.

Much has been written on the subject of 'over-criminalization.' It is not necessary to take a position on the familiar Devlin-Hart controversy to agree that in Canada, as in the United States, we have resorted to the criminal law as an instrument of social control to an extraordinary degree. Passing a law has been the easiest way of appearing to do something about situations that influential people have disapproved of; the range of subjects that have elicited this method of control is truly formidable. As early as 1934 (and perhaps earlier) the trend was criticized in the *Canadian Bar Review*:

When new situations present themselves, the legislators seem to feel impelled to deal with them by means of the criminal law. This is done according to no consistent scientific method, without a reliable foundation of knowledge as to the results of similar efforts in the past, and without due appreciation of the limitations on effective legal action by criminal procedure. Therefore every change is somewhat of a step in the dark, an experiment based on guesswork, rather than upon a sound judgment as to its probable utility or success.[1]

Much of the opposition to 'over-criminalization' has focused on the so-called crimes without victims: gambling, prostitution, abortion, homosexuality, and drug use. Since the offences in dispute all involve the willing exchange of desired goods and services, there are rarely complainants. As they are also transactions of low visibility, they necessitate expensive and often dubious methods of law enforcement, as well as being tempting sources of corruption. Hence, advocates of a changing morality have found allies among those seriously concerned with the quality of the administration of justice. But it should be noted that these offences are 'victimless' only in the sense that the harm is more remote, chancy, or debatable than in such traditional crimes as assault or burglary. Gambling may harm the family if it diverts enough of the wage-earner's income. Abortion may be interpreted as the murder of an unborn child. More relevant for the purposes of the present discussion is that harm may be done to the participant himself. The heroin addict acquires a dependence that drastically circumscribes his freedom of choice, whatever other, more uncertain, harms may ensue. Left to himself, the Skid Row alcoholic is exposed to a variety of physical dangers.

Given the commitment of our society to state intervention in matters of health, John Mill's position that the individual's 'own good, either physical or moral, is not a warrant' is not likely to be acceptable. 'Decriminalization' is a real possibility only if the criminal sanction is replaced by another form of intervention.

Examination of the problems involved in developing new social policies for dealing with Skid Row alcoholics and opiate addicts seems to indicate that initial commitment to a method of control – in this case the criminal justice system – tends to inhibit the discovery of feasible alternatives. As long as the legitimacy of the system of control is generally accepted and the visible manifestations of the disvalued behaviour are kept at a tolerable level, neither the motivation nor the resources to explore alternatives are likely to be forthcoming. When broader social changes cause the existing system to be challenged, the counterproposals tend to be based more on

1 Crouse, 'A Critique of Canadian Criminal Legislation,' (1934) 12 *Can. Bar Rev.* 601, at 603

faith than knowledge. Lack of the information necessary to assess the consequences of the various options supports a conservative bias in favour of modifications of the existing system rather than radical departures.

One of the endemic limitations of the criminal justice system as a method of control is accentuated in its dealings with Skid Row alcoholics and opiate addicts, namely, that it deals with deviance after the fact. Whatever the role of the law in general deterrence, the accused persons about whom the court has to make judgments are, by and large, those who have been deterred neither by the possibility of punishment nor by the complex of internal and external controls that keep most people sufficiently law-abiding or discreet to avoid the law's embrace. Skid Row alcoholics and opiate addicts bring out in extreme form the reactive rather than the preventive role in the law because they face the court at an advanced stage in their deviant careers. They are already dependent on the drug of their choice and have adopted a deviant life-style in which they associate chiefly with others like themselves. The probability that any of the sentencing options available to the court will either deter or rehabilitate is very small indeed.

The use of legal sanctions against narcotic addicts is ancillary to the efforts to prevent addiction by state control of the legal supply. The rigorous regulations applying to the importation, manufacture, and distribution of narcotic drugs are intended to eliminate non-medical use entirely. The criminal law is meant to reinforce the system of licensing and monitoring by providing heavy penalties for illegal transactions or possession. The result, as is well known, has been, not successful total prohibition, but a highly profitable illegal traffic, making criminal activity the only means through which most street addicts can raise the large amount of money necessary to support their habit. Estimates of the amount of gainful crime attributable to addicts have ranged from impressive to unbelievable. We will return later to the question of the effectiveness of the system in limiting and influencing the nature and distribution of opiate use.

State policies in regard to alcohol use have diverged increasingly from the system of narcotic control. When total prohibition was attempted, alcohol use had long been acceptable in large segments of society and had been integrated with a wide range of social activities. Moreover, strong economic interests had become associated with its promotion. Public familiarity with the effects of alcohol meant that any equivalent of the 'dope-fiend mythology' which served to justify drastic narcotic legislation was simply not credible, even at the height of the prohibition movement. Following the failure of prohibition, the tendency has been toward increasingly liberal alcohol-control policies, a change in which more widespread use has been both cause and effect.

Since the harmful effects of heavy alcohol use are well known, public policy has reflected a marked ambivalence. The façade of control in Canada and many other countries has taken the form of governmental regulation of manufacture, importation, and sales, coupled with highly profitable taxation and price markups – all with the avowed intent of limiting the 'abuse' of alcohol. To counterbalance the effects of advertising promotion by the liquor interests and greater availability through government stores and licensed outlets, as well as to satisfy the attendant concern over a public health problem, there has been increasing subsidization of research, treatment, and education intended to curb 'excessive' use by individuals. The policy has been based on the theory that the primary problem is alcohol addiction rather than other untoward effects of drinking; addiction, in turn, is considered to be due to the personal attributes of certain individuals which make them vulnerable to alcohol dependence. This view justifies concentrating on the vulnerable minority, while minimizing interference with 'normal' drinkers. It contrasts with the view, supported by considerable research, that there is no clear cut demarcation between those who are vulnerable and those who are not. It also contrasts with the research finding that the rate of alcoholism in a country is a function of the over-all level of consumption.[2] The latter views have had more influence in Scandinavian countries, where there has been a readiness to experiment with regulations regarding price, type and location of outlets, and other aspects of availability to influence levels and patterns of consumption.

In the alcohol control system, criminal sanctions have been employed mainly to deal with behavioural consequences of drinking that are defined as dangerous or offensive. In contrast to the narcotic field, the criminal sanctions related to illicit importation, manufacture, and sale are relatively unimportant because of legal availability. The ancient offence of being intoxicated in a public place is at the low end of the scale of harms punishable by law but accounts for a significant proportion of all arrests. Although the law, of course, applies equally to all citizens, it is in fact mainly the homeless, unattached drinkers of Skid Row who are vulnerable to arrest and, if arrested, to incarceration. In jurisdictions with zealous enforcement, chronic offenders may spend a large part of their time in jail.

2 See DeLint and Schmidt, 'Consumption Averages and Alcoholism Prevalence: A Brief Review of Epidemiological Investigations,' (1971), 66 *Brit. J. Addict.* 97.

'Life on the instalment plan' is an apt description used by the men themselves.

The use of criminal sanctions against addicts of both types has been challenged by the growing influence of the treatment ideology. What Francis Allen has called the 'rehabilitative ideal'[3] in its general application to the administration of criminal justice has been intensified in regard to heroin addicts and alcoholics by the more focused and widely accepted conception of addiction as a disease. The growth of the 'rehabilitative ideal' in its general application has been engendered by an alliance of those optimistic about the potentialities of developments in the behavioural and medical sciences with humanitarian critics intent on alleviating the punitiveness of criminal justice. Rehabilitation has generally been seen as synonymous with treatment based on the medical model. In practice, this has meant some variant of psychotherapy and only secondarily such practical help as the provision of basic skills and services. In short, it has been based on the highly debatable proposition that most offenders are sick people who can be re-established in society through psychiatric treatment.

In recent years, disillusionment with the treatment ideology has been expressed by responsible scholars.[4] Sound empirical studies have shown little reason for faith in existing treatment methods. It has been argued that the focus on treatment has discouraged exploration of other means of reducing crime that are capable of wider application. Enforced treatment in an institutional setting has been seen from a civil liberties viewpoint to be as punitive as undisguised imprisonment, but without the attendant legal safeguards. However, the treatment ideology has not been as subject to criticism in its application to opiate addiction and alcoholism. Because the ingestion of drugs and their effects on the organism are defining features, the medical model has special credibility in this area (although it has been the subject of intramural criticism by students of the subject).

First, let us examine the dilemma presented by the challenge to the use of criminal sanctions against Skid Row alcoholics. We will begin with a brief description of the 'revolving-door' system that prevailed in Toronto until recent unplanned changes in arrest and sentencing practices.[5] Although the law is phrased in universalistic terms, the homeless, indigent drinker is

3 Allen, 'Legal Values and the Rehabilitative Ideal,' in *The Borderland of Criminal Justice* (1964), at 25
4 See ibid; Anttila, 'Punishment Versus Treatment – Is There a Third Alternative?' (1972), 12 *Abst. Crim. and Pen.* 287.
5 The information is based on a study sponsored by the Alcoholism and Drug Addiction Research Foundation. See Giffen, 'The Revolving Door: A Functional Interpretation,' (1966), 3 *Can. Rev. of Soc. and Anth.* 154.

more likely to appear in public when drunk and more vulnerable to selective arrest practices. The result for the chronic offender is a continuing cycle of public intoxication, arrest, trial, incarceration, release into a Skid Row environment, and a return to drinking. The situation described is characteristic of a jurisdiction with relatively rigorous law enforcement and sentencing policies that lead to high probability of incarceration, practices which vary between jurisdictions and over time. In communities where the policy is to tolerate drunken behaviour on the part of homeless men as long as it is confined to clearly demarcated Skid Row enclaves, for example, the door to the jail revolves much less frequently.

The offender has traditionally been held in jail until his trial the next morning (bail reform has recently changed this practice). It is worth summarizing some of the unusual aspects of the trial procedure. Since the information is based on a study of the Toronto court that handled male drunk charges conducted over a decade ago, the procedures described do not reflect on the officials presently responsible.

The court, in effect, legitimated an unofficial social welfare system by means of a perfunctory ritual with a generally predictable outcome. The average length of trial was less than a minute from the time the accused entered the courtroom until he left. The physical setting – a small, tiled room with only two benches for spectators and witnesses – symbolized the lack of importance attached to the offence and the offenders. Lawyers appeared in only sixteen of the approximately eighteen thousand cases in the year of observation.

The police officer, who acted as prosecutor, had an extensive acquaintance with the large population of 'regulars' and consequently played an influential part in the proceedings. The seven magistrates who rotated duty were often dependent on his knowledge, especially when the identity or the record of the accused was in question, and occasionally consulted him about the advisability of a non-routine sentence. Sometimes he influenced the sentences by bringing certain facts about the accused to the attention of the court. Although his interventions often reflected sympathy for the accused, the combination of roles was a far cry from the ideal of the adversary system.

The procedures were attuned to the speedy disposition of cases in which guilt was implicitly assumed. When the accused reached the portable steel dock the clerk of the court quickly read a truncated version of the charge. On only 5 per cent of the court days did the clerk state the full substance of the information. The rest of the time he either said: 'You are charged with being drunk in a public place,' or simply, 'You are charged with being drunk.' Certain magistrates had instructed the clerk to use the shorter form on the grounds that the term 'public place' only confused the defendants. In 96 per cent of the cases this immediately elicited the expected guilty plea.

Those who answered 'not guilty' were treated as if they had committed an error that they should be given an opportunity to rectify. When the last case was heard the prosecutor went to the cells and asked if anybody wanted to change his plea to 'guilty'; over one-fifth of eligibles did so. Another opportunity was presented to the remainder when they reappeared for trial and approximately one-quarter did so. In the end, only 292 cases were contested, and of these only twenty-two were dismissed.

Sentence was usually pronounced immediately after the clerk read the accused's record of convictions over the previous twelve months, without time-consuming deliberations or exchanges. Each of the seven magistrates had developed his own scale of penalties, graded primarily in accordance with the number of previous convictions. The 'individualization' of sentencing that took place in a minority of cases was usually a paternalistic response to a plea for leniency on the grounds of hardship. Paradoxically, the most frequent plea for leniency put forward and granted was that the accused deserved a 'break' because of the number of lengthy terms he had served in recent months. The right to a 'break' every so often appeared to be an unwritten rule familiar to all the regular participants.

A striking irregularity in sentencing was that many of the penalties deviated from the statutory prescription, usually on the side of leniency, until an amendment to the Liquor Control Act legalized the practice of the court by removing mandatory jail sentences for multiple offenders and minimum fines and default terms for others. A large proportion of the suspended sentences were also non-statutory, either because a minimum was prescribed or because the offender had previous convictions. In effect, the court reflected public opinion rather than the law and in doing so anticipated statutory changes.

The paradox of central importance to the operation of the revolving-door system was that although most of the penalties were fines, most of the chronic offenders served default jail terms. The proportion unable to pay their fines in court ranged from 40 per cent, for men up for their first offence within twelve months, to 96 per cent, for those up for a sixth or subsequent offence. The overwhelming majority of the chronic offenders could expect to spend up to thirty days in jail several times a year.

The degree of suffering involved has to be seen in terms of relative deprivation. For most chronic offenders jail was not highly distasteful in comparison to the life of chaotic drinking and uncertain subsistence on

Skid Row. In the Toronto Jail many of the 'regulars' came to acquire a right to one of the wide range of housekeeping and maintenance jobs with its unofficial rewards, returning to it each time they were admitted. Mutual dependence and long acquaintance tended to foster sympathetic relationships between many regulars and staff members. Even men less integrated in the jail system found some satisfaction in the orderly existence and assured food and shelter.

The revolving-door system has both beneficial and harmful effects. On the favourable side, it gives the men some protection from the consequences of prolonged heavy drinking sprees, during which they eat little or nothing. Police intervention shortens their sprees, as well as protecting them from possible injury. The jail term is a period of recuperation; nutritious meals, regular hours, and total abstinence help to prevent some of the physical damage associated with prolonged heavy drinking.

But the system also has a number of unfavourable consequences. The most obvious is that it fosters continued recidivism: once a man has entered the revolving door, the probability of his escaping is small, except through death or extreme infirmity. Since jails do not pretend to rehabilitate, the man leaves as he entered, without resources and with no place to go but back to Skid Row. Indeed, jail serves as a meeting place and centre of communication that reinforces his integration in Skid Row society. It has also been hypothesized that jail life weakens any motivation to control his drinking behaviour by complementing his Skid Row existence, alternating periods of orderly living with periods of licence. A jail term may serve as a deterrent to an offender in the early stages, but it also is likely to create a vicious circle in that it decreases his probability of maintaining a job or residence and brings him into the company of Skid Row alcoholics.

What are the alternatives in public policy to the revolving-door system? One is simply to leave the Skid Row alcoholic to his own devices, to do away with the offence and provide no facilities expressly for this type of alcoholic. The common objection to such a policy is the harm that would come to the homeless drunk if there were no public caretakers. Officials of the criminal justice system have generally been favourable to the idea of 'decriminalizing' public drunkenness but with the proviso that somebody else should take care of the homeless alcoholic. Given the undignified and time-consuming nature of the task, it is not surprising that they should be willing to transfer the responsibility to the health and welfare system. The US Supreme Court has opposed discontinuing the present system in the absence of some alternative. In the case of *Powell* v *Texas*, Mr Justice Marshall stated in his majority opinion: 'However, facilities for the attempted treatment of indigent alcoholics are woefully lacking throughout the country. It would be tragic to return large numbers of helpless, sometimes dangerous and frequently unsanitary inebriates to the streets of our cities without even the opportunity to sober up adequately which a brief jail term provides.'[6]

Detoxication centres under public health auspices have been the most commonly proposed replacement for the drunk tank. An experimental unit operated in Toronto by the Addiction Research Foundation between 1968 and 1970 proved that expensive medical staffing was unnecessary because physical complications were rare. Consequently, the units recently set up in Toronto and those planned for other centres are manned by non-medical staffs. However, such units depend on some arrangement for rescuing the homeless drunks from the streets. In Ontario the compromise has been to continue to depend on the police; the Liquor Control Act has been amended to empower the police officers to escort public inebriates to a detoxication centre in lieu of laying an information. It is a mixed system in the sense that the police, at their discretion or because beds are sometimes unavailable, may use the criminal justice system for some inebriates and the detoxication centre for others.

The objection to detoxication centres in the absence of more long-term treatment and caretaking facilities is that they tend to become revolving doors themselves, but rotating even more rapidly. The prescribed stay is only a few days, and experience has shown that many men leave after a few hours. The health protection of the longer jail term is lost, and the motivation of the police to operate a taxi service may be weakened.

However, proposals for additional facilities reveal that it is easy to dream up institutional arrangements but difficult to prescribe the substance of programs that carry any assurance of effectiveness. Among the suggestions for institutions have been out-patient clinics in Skid Row, farms and work colonies, halfway houses, small 'self-help' residences, foster homes, and sheltered workshops. The goals have varied from a responsible, sober, productive life in the community to permanent residence in a protected setting.

The lack of substance and assurance in these proposals reflects both the weaknesses of the medical model and the absence of known techniques for dealing with persons with many problems. Experience has shown that the conventional 'talking' therapies aimed at drinking problems have little success with homeless alcoholics. The simple resolve to give up drinking

6 *Powell* v *Texas*, (1968) 88A S.Ct. 2145, at 2152; 392 U.S. 514, at 528

does not overcome the apparently hopeless obstacles to securing a job, a home, and a stable set of relationships outside of Skid Row. Commitment to the medical model makes it difficult for those responsible for social policy to think in terms of compromise solutions that recognize intractable elements in the problem.

The issues surrounding the control of opiate addiction can be dealt with briefly because of the publicity the subject has received in recent years. Challenges to the monopoly of control through the criminal justice system have generated an intense controversy that has made difficult any objective assessment of the claims made for various modes of control. The problem has been compounded by the very different beliefs about addiction and addicts associated with ideological commitment to the law enforcement approach or its alternatives. The opposition to shifting control of narcotic addicts to the medical profession is in marked contrast to the willingness to extrude the homeless alcoholic from the criminal justice system. This does not mean that proponents of the law enforcement approach have opposed all treatment for addicts – the equivalent of denigrating motherhood – but they have demanded that it take the form of long-term commitment to an institution, for them a functional equivalent of imprisonment.

The strength of the law enforcement position is explained in part by the historical background. In Canada, as in the United States, the definition of opiate addiction as a problem for the criminal justice system began with the first narcotics legislation prior to the first world war and became entrenched with the elimination of any significant role for the medical profession.[7] Growth of the enforcement hegemony was supported by the set of beliefs that has been called the 'dope fiend mythology.' A credulous public, unfamiliar with addicts, was willing to believe the worst, especially when it was associated with anti-Chinese sentiment. The dope fiend was portrayed as given to crimes of violence, morally degenerate, anxious to convert non-users, and subject to irreversible physical damage. With the virtual disappearance of addicts who had been innocently addicted through the ready availability of medicines containing opiates, the myth came to embody the belief that most addicts were recruited from the ranks of criminals. With public backing, the enforcement network was able to proliferate and secure legislation that extended the range of offences and proscribed drugs, increased the penalties, and gave the police extraordinary powers of search. The supplying of drugs to an addict by a physician purely for the purposes of satisfying his addiction came to be accepted as

7 See Cook, *Variations in Response to Illegal Drug Use* (1970) (unpublished M. Phil. thesis, University of Toronto).

illegal after changes in the wording of the Act and the successful prosecution of a number of flagrant prescription-pedlars. In the absence of challenges in the higher courts that might have led to a wider interpretation of professional discretion, the de facto ban on the provision of maintenance doses of any opiates continued until the period following the Narcotic Control Act of 1961. The removal of the definition of the rights of physicians from the Act to the Regulations opened the way for quietly negotiated change, leading to the authorization of methadone maintenance by clinics and private physicians.

When criticisms of the North American system began to emerge, the most clear-cut proposal for change – referred to as the 'British system' – was that addicts should be provided with drugs. The British approach developed from difficulties in interpreting the rights of physicians under the Dangerous Drugs Act of 1920. The government appointed a committee, headed by an eminent physician, to make recommendations clarifying the conditions under which physicians might legally prescribe narcotics. The most significant recommendation was that physicians be allowed to supply drugs to addicts in those apparently incurable cases where the individual was unable to lead a normal life without a regular minimum dose.[8] The recommendation was accepted and became the distinguishing characteristic of British policy. Advocates of the British approach argued that furnishing maintenance doses under medical supervision would eliminate the illegal traffic by drying up demand and addicts would no longer be driven to crime to pay for the high cost of illegal drugs. The dangers to health due to malnutrition, infection from dirty needles, and inadvertent overdoses would disappear. The addict subculture would lose its main reason for existence – the important relationship would be doctor and patient. Underlying this optimism was, of course, a strong moral aversion to the punishment of addicts.

Although the extreme counterarguments came from enforcement officials, others with a sympathetic interest in the problem have had questions about the suitability of the British approach to the North American situation. Given the enforcement authorities' conception of the addict, it was logical that they should see maintenance doses as compounding the problem. Drugs supplied legally would simply increase the total supply. Since addicts took drugs for their euphoric effects, they would supplement their legal supply with drugs from the illegal market. That addicts would be

8 Ministry of Health, Departmental Committee on Morphine and Heroin Addiction, *Report* (1926), at 20

enabled to lead normal lives was countered by the assertion that they had been criminals prior to addiction and would continue to be, with or without legal drugs. Since drug use was believed to be physically damaging, supplying drugs legally was seen as morally equivalent to dispensing free drinks to alcoholics.

Less partisan questions were raised about the comparability of the addiction situation in Great Britain with that of North America. Did the British approach work because the addict population was small and made up largely of therapeutically addicted middle-class persons? Did British social standards successfully discourage the spread of hedonistic drug use? Data from subsequent studies and reports supported the view that the addiction situation had been significantly different. At the time the control system came into effect in Great Britain opiate addiction was relatively rare – the Dangerous Drugs Act was meant to honour an obligation under the Treaty of Versailles. Until recent years, known addicts never numbered more than a few hundred. According to one writer,[9] an estimated 85 per cent were therapeutic addicts, 10 per cent were doctors and nurses, and 5 per cent had become addicted through undetermined means. Therapeutic addicts tended to be middle aged, distributed widely over the country, and not part of a deviant subculture. The Brain committee of 1958, reviewing the operation of the system, concluded that it had been satisfactory and attributed the continuing minor nature of the problem to 'social attitudes to the observance of the law in general and to the taking of dangerous drugs in particular.'[10]

Changes in the addict population in the 1960s support the proposition that some of the apparent success of this system was related to the social situation. The Brain committee was reconvened in 1964[11] because of reports of a rapid increase in heroin and cocaine use, which they concluded had indeed taken place, particularly among the younger age groups. The source of drugs in their view was mainly a large increase in prescriptions by a very few doctors and not an illegal traffic. The committee proposed that the furnishing of drugs to addicts should be restricted to the staffs of special treatment centres. The centres were not intended to be simply dispensaries; the opportunity was to be used to help addicts with their social and

9 Willis, 'Drug Addiction – The Extent and Nature of the Problem,' (1968), 84 *Transactions of the Medical Society of London*, 74
10 Ministry of Health, Department of Health for Scotland, *Report of the Interdepartmental Committee on Drug Addiction*, (1961), at 9
11 Ministry of Health, Scottish Home and Health Department, *Drug Addiction; The Second Report of the Interdepartmental Committee on Drug Addiction* (1965)

occupational adjustment, as well as to encourage them to give up drug use. The committee emphatically rejected the crime control model; strict legal regulations that would prevent or discourage addicts from obtaining supplies from legitimate sources would, in the committee's view, lead to the development of an organized illicit traffic. However, doctors were to be required to report heroin and cocaine addicts to a central authority. These recommendations were embodied in the Dangerous Drugs Act of 1967.

It is too early to judge the effects of the changes in the British system on the total problem. The new users are mostly non-therapeutic addicts, members of a youth culture in search of hedonistic experience. This raises the old question whether or not they will be content with maintenance doses or will seek more from other sources, thus encouraging an illegal traffic and developing a full-fledged addict subculture.

Organized opposition to the law enforcement monopoly emerged in Canada when the Community Chest of Vancouver, in co-operation with the British Columbia Medical Association, formed the Committee on the Prevention of Narcotic Addiction. In 1952, the committee submitted a brief to the minister of health and welfare recommending drug education, experimental treatment programmes, provincial clinics providing maintenance doses with a view to cure, and increased penalties for large-scale traffickers. Two years later, the government appointed the Senate Special Committee on the Traffic in Narcotic Drugs in Canada.[12] After hearing evidence from witnesses representing a variety of viewpoints, the special committee came up with recommendations favouring the law enforcement approach – more vigorous enforcement and heavier penalties – but also recommended commitment for treatment on a compulsory or voluntary basis with provision for post-discharge control, including long-term probation. Proposals to provide maintenance doses to addicts were rejected. These (and other) recommendations were embodied in the Narcotic Control Act of 1961.[13] The treatment provision – still unproclaimed – took the form of indefinite commitment of convicted persons judged to be addicts to a facility within the penitentiary system.

Drug control policies again came up for official re-evaluation with the appointment of the Le Dain commission in 1969. Although prompted mainly by concern about the new class of youthful, middle-class users of hallucinogenic drugs, all non-medical use of drugs was included in the terms of reference. The commissioners' recommendations for an over-all

12 Senate, Special Committee, *The Traffic in Narcotic Drugs in Canada* (1955)
13 Now the Narcotic Control Act, R.S.C. 1970, C.N-1

system for dealing with opiate addiction, which would indicate their view of the role of criminal sanctions, have yet to be published,[14] although a report on treatment methods has appeared. The hearings and briefs manifested the proliferation of viewpoints, proposals, and experiments in recent years.

However, the diverse proposals of the current debate all appear to be variants or combinations of four main types. The most easily disposed of is the extreme civil libertarian position of making opiates freely available on the same basis as alcohol. Few responsible professionals would accept the equation of heroin and alcohol because of the high addiction propensity of the opiates and the rapid escalation of tolerance. Despite evidence that active proselytization is not characteristic of addicts, there is no way of predicting how widespread addiction would become if the sale of drugs were legalized.

At the other extreme is the proposal to continue to rely on criminal sanctions on the ground that the system has kept down the level of addiction and would be able to do even more with additional resources. The degree of 'success' depends on the criteria. The rate of addiction undoubtedly declined in the period following the introduction of the narcotic control system because of the reduction in the large number of persons addicted to medicines containing opiates and the gradual disappearance of the opium smoker. Law enforcement efforts changed opiate addiction from a widely diffused phenomenon to one concentrated in the lower socioeconomic areas of large cities, those areas in which the necessary criminal networks could survive. Hence, the use of criminal sanctions could be interpreted as highly successful in Prince Edward Island but not in Vancouver. Although there has been a continuous growth in the resources devoted to narcotic law enforcement since this pattern became established, drug use has shown an embarrassing tendency to vary independently. An epidemic increase in heroin addiction took place in the United States after the second world war, and the large increase in marijuana use in both countries in the sixties took place within the same set of laws. After a long period of relative stability, the number of narcotic users known to the Canadian authorities is reported to have risen dramatically since 1969 and the population of users is known to have become more widely dispersed. Within the limiting and channeling effects of the law enforcement system, other social variables apparently exert a powerful influence.

14 See the *Final Report of the Commission of Inquiry into the Non-Medical Use of Drugs* (1973), released after this paper was prepared.

Criticisms of the effect of the crime control model on the addicts themselves have already been alluded to: the need to resort to crime to raise the money and the dangers to health and life of using unpredictable doses under unsanitary conditions. While it might seem logical from a humanitarian viewpoint to lessen the suffering of the addict by focusing law enforcement efforts on the trafficker, much of the reported efficacy of the present approach rests on the fact that users are much easier to catch and convict than traffickers and when traffickers are put out of business the high profits quickly attract replacements. In the words of an RCMP officer testifying before the Senate Committee in 1955:

It would appear that a continuous and vigorous attack on the traffickers is not the answer to the suppression of drug addiction, although this course is absolutely necessary. The answer to the problem would seem to lie in the opposite direction, that is, vigorous action against the addicts. As long as the addict creates a demand and is willing to pay high prices for his drugs, the more important criminal element will supply it much the same as other types of criminal commodities or services are provided, despite police action.[15]

Law enforcement concentration on the demand side appears to be inevitable as long as the continuing international efforts to dry up the supplies at the source are unsuccessful.

Treatment of the addict with a view to bringing about total abstinence, the third approach, has the attraction of reconciling the value-conflict implicit in punishing the individual for a condition defined as an illness while retaining the medical ideal of full recovery. Unfortunately, experience with existing treatment methods gives no guidance as to how this is to be achieved on a wide scale, nor any assurance that it can be. The following statement from the Le Dain commission reflects the disenchantment with methods that have been tried:

Thus, many different types of treatments have been proposed and are being employed in an effort to cope with opiate dependence, including prolonged psychoanalysis, therapeutic communities, counselling, compulsory confinement and surveillance by probation officers. However, all forms of treatment have so far met with very limited success ... Several investigators have studied samples of several hundred voluntary first admissions to opiate withdrawal programs. The relapse rate to narcotics varied from 90 to 95 per cent.[16]

15 Senate, supra note 12, at 399–400
16 *A Report of the Commission of Inquiry into the Non-Medical Use of Drugs: Treatment* (1972), at 10–11

One author of follow-up studies is quoted as concluding: 'In short, the conventional medical model for the treatment of narcotic addiction is simply not effective.'[17] The claims of therapeutic communities – some run by ex-addicts and others supervised by professional personnel – are difficult to assess because of the lack of follow-up studies. A survey of therapeutic communities in New York City, cited in the Le Dain commission report, concluded that the percentage who maintain a drug-free state was too small to justify the high cost of such programmes.

The findings of the experimental treatment programme conducted at Matsqui, the British Columbia institution that is part of the penitentiary service, are especially ironical in view of the unproclaimed treatment section in the 1961 Narcotic Control Act. An experimental group was given treatment within the therapeutic community, while another group that was given no treatment served as a control. The results showed that the treated group became more successful drug addicts. They were able to use the skills and understanding they had received in treatment to earn more from illegal activities than the control group, and their total opiate use was higher.[18]

The fourth approach, supplying maintenance doses to addicts, assumes that total abstinence is not a realistic goal for many and that the use of criminal sanctions is, at best, not sufficiently successful to justify the suffering caused the addict. Although the Le Dain commission recommends continuation of all the conventional therapies, it concludes that, 'for better or for worse, methadone maintenance provides to date the cheapest and most effective weapon we have for dealing with large-scale heroin dependence.'[19] However, evidence from the report indicates that the methadone maintenance schemes, even if provided on a wide scale, are not likely to eliminate illicit heroin use. Some existing programmes are found to have drop-out rates as high as 50 per cent. A significant number of addicts seem unwilling to forgo the euphoric effects of heroin and perhaps the various secondary gains of life in the addict subculture. Presumably many other addicts, for these and additional reasons, would not enrol in a programme at all. The contention of sceptics that transplanting the British system would mean supplementing illicit supplies and thus increase use is seen to have some grounds in the commission's finding that a considerable amount of methadone has been leaking into illegal markets, particularly through the prescribing of the drug to addicts by private physicians in the absence of strict controls.

17 Ibid, at 11
18 Ibid, at 12–13
19 Ibid, at 30

This examination of proposals to replace the criminal justice system with other methods of dealing with opiate addicts and Skid Row alcoholics has, of necessity, been sketchy; it is perhaps adequate to illustrate the difficulty of finding workable alternatives in the present state of knowledge. This is accounted for, in part, by the absence of strong motivation to study other possibilities during the period when the use of criminal sanctions was the generally acceptable solution. But it is also apparent that there are inherent difficulties in bringing about the total abstinence and normal living that are the goals of the rehabilitative ideal. Sufficient research has been done in the treatment of addicts to justify doubts about the yield of greater efforts along the same lines. Proposals which accept a large degree of intractability appear to have a realistic basis.

Whatever the intellectual merits of various proposals, actual changes in public policies will, of course, largely be shaped by political realities. Public conceptions of the dangers of narcotic drug use, fostered by the labelling of addiction as seriously criminal, are likely to rule out any significant abandonment of criminal sanctions. Once law enforcement has been established through usage as the method of dealing with what comes to be defined as a serious danger, public resistance to change tends to create an institutional inertia. Governmental concessions to critics are likely to take the form of more liberal provisions for experimental treatment and maintenance programmes within the framework of the existing system. Since public opinion, in contrast, appears to be favourable to doing away with punishment of homeless alcoholics, political considerations will focus on the cost of alternative health and welfare facilities. Since the problems of indigent alcoholics are not high on the scale of social priorities, the facilities provided are not likely to be of a size or type that would greatly improve their lot in life. And in many less prosperous jurisdictions the machinery of criminal justice is likely to continue by default to be the mode of official intervention for a long time to come.

JAMES GIFFEN, a graduate of the University of Toronto, is a professor and former chairman, Department of Sociology, University of Toronto. He has been closely associated with the Centre of Criminology and the Addiction Research Foundation and has contributed to publications on a range of subjects, including the legal profession, criminal statistics, and alcoholism and drug addiction.

DONALD DEWEES

The courts and economic regulation

This paper will examine the role that courts have played in the past and
can play in future in regulating private economic behaviour. We will consider the degree to which the courts as an institution are suited to this task
and compare their performance with that of administrative agencies in
regulating corporate and individual conduct. Particular attention will be
paid to the degree of punishment imposed upon those who do not comply
with the law, the effectiveness of this punishment in securing the desired
behaviour, and the definition of punishment which can give some assurance of being effective.

COURTS VS REGULATORY AGENCIES

In Canada substantial limitations on private activity are imposed by court
interpretation and enforcement of common-law principles which have
developed over many years both here and in Britain. If a legislature wishes
to modify private economic activity further, it must choose between providing a general mandate to a regulatory agency that will develop rules and
enforce them and specifying prohibited conduct directly in the legislation,
leaving enforcement to the judicial process.

The regulation of industrial structure and conduct through the anti-
combines laws offers an example of judicial enforcement of direct legislation. The objectives of anti-combines laws include controlling the economic and social power wielded by firms in concentrated industries.
The mechanism to achieve this control is regulation of industrial structure

and conduct by limiting certain pricing behaviour, mergers, and interfirm agreements. These laws are not self-enforcing, but require the government or private citizens to observe industrial behaviour and prosecute in court those whose conduct appears to violate the legislative standards. The impact of such laws depends largely upon the success achieved in prosecution of these court cases and upon the penalties imposed.

Environmental protection is an area where legislation alone is not sufficient to translate the public will into effective action. Environmental legislation frequently creates an administrative body to set standards and determine the extent of compliance with these standards, as is done in the Ontario Environmental Protection Act.[1] The effectiveness of the administrative body is commonly measured by the number of pollutors prosecuted administratively or in court for their violation of the legislation and standards. Canadian courts are thus frequently involved in the regulation of pollution emissions, whether through actions under the common law or prosecution under regulatory statutes.

Regulatory agencies have been favourably regarded during the last half century because of their ability to develop expertise in the area over which they have control. With a narrow mandate, an agency can hire specialists who understand the technical problems in the area and can therefore deal with them more reasonably than a court of law. Administrative agencies may also adopt procedures that are far less cumbersome than those applied in the judiciary for hearing evidence and deciding disputes. The agency can undertake independent studies of problems within its jurisdiction and modify its rules or regulations in accordance with the findings of these studies, giving itself a degree of flexibility unknown to the courts.

A system of judicial enforcement, on the other hand, is constrained to operate with the original legislation or the common law unless the legislature returns to the problem to amend that legislation. Because judges and courts tend on the whole to be conservative, this system is not particularly flexible or responsive to social change unless the legislature acts. Furthermore, cases in a particular area such as anti-combines may be raised in many courts. Since each court handles a variety of cases it cannot possibly become expert in any particular field. This has led in numerous cases to decisions less astute than might have been desired, in part because technical aspects of the problem were not fully understood. The courts will be

---

1 The Environmental Protection Act 1971, Stats. Ont. 1971, c 86, as amended by Stats. Ont. 1972, c 1, s.69, and Stats. Ont. 1972, c 106

bound by traditional legal rules of evidence and procedures which can lead to extended periods of fact-finding and trials of long duration.

Still, the advantages are not entirely on the side of the administrative agency. The rules of evidence are used in courts of law because centuries of experience both here and in Britain have demonstrated these rules to be necessary and effective in obtaining the most reliable possible evidence and sifting through a mass of conflicting claims to ascertain the truth. Thus the speed and simplicity of administrative proceedings are obtained at the risk of sacrificing some accuracy and justice. Furthermore, courts, while conservative, are not hopelessly inflexible, and there are examples of substantial social change resulting from judicial reinterpretation of existing law.[2] Administrative agencies frequently suffer from the need to obtain experts from the regulated industry itself. When there is a substantial flow of personnel between the agency and the industry, it is not surprising to find the agency's regulatory zeal somewhat diminished.[3] In fact, the numerous problems of regulatory agencies in the United States prompted one commissioner to state, 'my experience on the Civil Aeronautics Board has convinced me that an independent regulatory commission is not competent in these days to regulate a vital national industry in the public interest.'[4]

The gulf between enforcement by administrative agency and the judiciary need not be as wide as is generally assumed. If the area of regulation involves complex technical issues, it is possible to establish a specialized court which hears all cases in that field. This allows the court to develop its own expertise without giving up the procedural safeguards inherent in a judicial proceeding. In addition, it is possible for the court to hire experts of its own to give special guidance in complicated cases. Some precedent for this is offered by Judge Wyzanski's use of an economic clerk as a special assistant in the *United Shoe* case.[5] Alternatively, one might

2 See *Brown v Board of Education of Topeka*, (1954), 347 U.S. 483, which held that separate schools for negroes were inherently unequal and therefore denied the equal protection of the laws guaranteed by the fourteenth amendment. This specifically overruled contrary language in *Plessy v Ferguson*, (1896) 163 U.S. 537.

3 A number of economic studies have suggested that the net long-run effect of various regulatory agencies is negligible because of a tendency to promote, not restrain, the industry. See MacAvoy ed, *The Crisis of the Regulatory Commissions* (1970).

4 Memorandum of Louis J. Hector to President Eisenhower, 10 Sept. 1959, reprinted in Gellhorn and Byse *Administrative Law: Cases and Comments* (4th ed, 1960), at 56

5 *United States v United Shoe Machinery Corp.*, (D. Mass. 1953) 110 F. Supp. 295, aff'd *per curiam* (1954) 347 U.S. 521

establish an administrative tribunal but circumscribe its activities with procedures very similar to those which would exist in a court of law.[6]

Whether enforcement of the public will is through the administrative or judicial process, it is necessary to determine when firms or individuals are not in compliance with the law. It is also necessary to establish punishments that will encourage compliance yet not impose unreasonable burdens on offenders. We will now consider some experience offered by the courts in establishing levels of punishment for various cases, and their implications for effective control of private economic activity.

JUDICIAL ACTION: COMMON LAW ENVIRONMENTAL PROTECTION

For decades, and even centuries, we have relied primarily upon the common law to protect environmental quality. The fact that since the early sixties Canada, along with most of the industrialized world, has become seriously concerned about environmental problems suggests that this protection has not been altogether satisfactory. This dissatisfaction results from permitting unnecessary degradation of environmental quality and not efficiently distributing the burden of protecting the environment where adequate quality has been achieved.

If all pollution problems arose in situations with a single pollutor and a single pollutee, each with equal bargaining power, then it seems probable that negotiations could lead to a satisfactory resolution of most such conflicts.[7] If the law clearly specified allowable pollution levels, the parties could use that law as a starting point for negotiations; if it appeared advantageous to allow more or less than the statutory amount, they could so agree between them and compensate with monetary payments. If pollution were entirely prohibited, the pollutor might bribe the pollutee to accept a small amount of pollution, just as a supplier of coal gives up that coal in exchange for a sufficient amount of money. If the law allowed pollution, then the pollutee might bribe the pollutor to emit less smoke, paying him an amount sufficient to compensate the pollutor for any costs for reducing his

6 A faltering step in this direction was taken in defining the Competitive Practices Tribunal in Bill C-256 (The Competition Act, 3d session, 28th Parliament, 19–20 Elizabeth 1970–1), which was subsequently withdrawn. The latest version, Bill C-2, introduced in the fall of 1974, does not contain some of the more interesting features of Bill C-256 referred to in this paper.

7 The seminal article on this point is Coase, 'The Problem of Social Cost,' (1960), 3 *J. Law and Econ.* 1.

emissions. In a world consisting only of two-party situations the role of the court would be to determine how much pollution the law allowed in each case and settle the facts if these were in dispute. If a pollutor chose to ignore that law and the pollution damage was substantial, the pollutee would have a sufficient incentive to incur the legal costs necessary to enforce his rights.

Such a situation is analogous to one involving the large electrical manufacturers and purchasers of generators, motors, and heavy equipment in the United States in the early sixties. While the total number of parties involved was substantial, most of the claims arose out of simple two-party contracts in which Westinghouse, General Electric, or others had sold equipment to an identified purchaser. When price-fixing was uncovered in federal criminal actions, the purchasers reminded the sellers of the civil provisions of the anti-trust laws through a number of treble damage suits which cost the manufacturers over $500 million.[8] The financial rewards to individual plaintiffs were sufficient to warrant the costs and risks of civil litigation.

Most pollution problems, however, involve many pollutees, so that it is not an individual but a group or public problem. Environmental quality is therefore not a private but a public good. In such cases individual action cannot significantly affect the result and is not forthcoming. Suppose that a single factory in town emits smoke from a tall smoke stack. If every resident of the town suffers a small amount of pollution damage, he has little incentive to sue the factory, even though the total damage to all citizens may be quite substantial. The small harm to the individual may not compensate him for the time, trouble, and expense of litigation. This is analogous to the more common case of monopolization or price-fixing at the retail level, where the product is small and the damage to any purchaser insignificant. The record contains few cases in which individual consumers have brought price-fixing suits because of the increase in cost for toothpaste, soap, or other relatively small items whose prices are raised by actions which may be violations of the anti-trust or anti-combines laws.

The resistance by the pollutor to an individual suit would be substantial because the loss of one such suit might lead to judgment in favour of many other similarly situated plaintiffs. Potential plaintiffs tend to forgo such litigation since the private benefits are small compared to the probable private costs. The result is usually that no action is taken. Those who do

8 The consent decree in the criminal actions is in *U.S.* v *Westinghouse Electric Corp.*, CCH *1963 Trade Cases* 70,633. The civil suits involved many separate actions, some of which are discussed in Alioto, 'The Economics of a Treble Damage Case,' (1966), 32 *Antitrust L.J.* 87.

sue are often not motivated by their own private interest, which is quite small, but by matters of principle or missionary zeal. The results of this system are both unpredictable and erratic.[9] Whether a pollutor will face a private suit depends, not on the total damage from his emissions, but on whether his activities happen to catch the attention of a citizens' group or environmental organization. Among equally situated pollutors, some will become defendants and others will not. This is not an efficient basis for planning capital investment in pollution-control facilities. It also means that the results do not necessarily reflect the severity of the problems and many pollutors may remain untouched while others suffer great crusades.

The plaintiff in a common law action has other problems. He must prove he has been harmed, and in general this requires, not simply a moderate aesthetic degradation, but some specific and quantifiable loss.[10] Yet medical knowledge is not sufficient today to prove that an increase of a certain pollutant at a moderate level will necessarily cause particular diseases.[11] Nor is it easy to show in all but the most severe and exceptional cases that reduced crop yields, discolouration of paint, or other forms of physical damage have been caused by the defendant's emissions. For the typical urban resident who would rather see and breathe cleaner air, proof of harm is almost impossible.

Even where damage can be shown, it is necessary to demonstrate that the defendant is responsible for that harm. In the case of a single pollutor, as in the one-factory town, this may not be difficult. In the more typical urban setting, however, if many sources emit the pollutant in question, attributing specific harm to a single defendant may be extremely difficult. Complex scientific investigations may be required, necessitating long delays and great expenditures.

A final problem with common law litigation is that in the environmental field no less than in anti-combines, complex economic issues may be raised. Controlling pollution is really a problem in resource allocation. The scarce resource is the capability of the atmosphere or the water to carry off waste products from domestic and industrial activity. In general, we allow the private economic system to allocate scarce resources such as coal, iron, and timber, subject to varying degrees of governmental intervention,

9 Johnson, 'The Changing Role of the Courts in Water-Quality Management,' in Campbell and Sylvester eds, *Water Resources Management and Public Policy* (1968) 196, at 200
10 Prosser, 'Private Action for Public Nuisance,' (1966), 52 *Va. L. R.* 997, at 1007
11 Few studies offer solid numerical relationships between pollution and health. For a sophisticated statistical study see Lave and Seskin, 'Air Pollution and Human Health,' (1970), 169 *Science* 723.

on the ground that the competitive market system will make the most efficient allocation of these resources. Because markets do not exist for the use of air and water as carriers of waste, the courts have had to devise rules for allocating this resource on an ad hoc basis.

While courts are well designed to investigate matters of fact and examine past actions, they are not well adapted to creating rules that implement economic concepts such as efficient resource allocation. The laws of riparian rights and of prior appropriation, which have developed for the allocation of water use, have in fact settled disputes over water rights but do not appear to have promoted the efficient allocation of water among its many competing uses. The balancing of benefits from pollution reduction against the possibility that the pollutor may have to raise his price, or even shut down his plant, with the resulting economic repercussions, requires expertise far beyond that available to most courts.[12] Determining the impact of a particular pollution control order might well require a complete industry study, of which few have been sponsored by governments in all of Canada and none has been commissioned by a Canadian court.

It thus appears that judicial enforcement of common law rights is not a particularly effective means of protecting environmental quality, any more than it was an effective means of protecting the public against the evils of monopoly and big business. This has to do as much with the particular characteristics of environmental problems as it does with deficiencies in the courts themselves. Even an American trial lawyer who has met with substantial success in prosecuting individual environmental suits against pollutors and pollutants has conceded that litigation was not a solution to environmental problems but 'a means of presenting evidence to the conscience of the community' and has urged that legislation be drafted.[13] Thus, if we are to provide a 'public good' through government direction of private economic activity, legislation will be necessary, combined with judicial or administrative enforcement. This raises the problem of designing penalties to ensure adequate compliance with the law.

PROBLEMS OF ENFORCING LEGISLATION OR REGULATIONS

Legislation or regulations prohibiting certain forms of conduct may elicit three kinds of response from the public. Some portion of the population will be governed primarily by a sense of moral duty and will obey the law simply

12 See Meyers and Tarlock *Water Resource Management* (1971) chap. 5A.
13 Yannacone jr, 'Environmental Litigation,' *1971 Proceedings of the section of Insurance, Negligence and Compensation Law of the American Bar Association* 320

because it is law, regardless of enforcement. Another segment of the population may act irrationally or perversely or in the heat of passion, so that on them the law has no effect whatsoever. Those who are ignorant of the law are similarly unaffected.

There will, in general, be a third category: persons whose behaviour is governed primarily by some rational consideration. Such people will weigh the costs and the benefits of a particular action, including violation of the new law. If their expected gains from violation are greater than the expected costs then violation is profitable and probable.[14] The history of compliance with laws generally and pollution control laws particularly suggests that an effective law must deal adequately with this group. To influence this third group's behaviour it is necessary to have an enforcement mechanism such that the costs of violation are greater than the gains which may be reaped. The costs will involve the probability of conviction for violating the law and the severity of the penalty imposed. The gains from violation will presumably be the added revenue which can be gathered in the case of price-fixing or monopolization or avoiding the expenses associated with meeting a pollution control law.

The importance in this calculation of the probability of being convicted must be emphasized. Suppose that a law prohibits emission of a certain pollutant and specifies a one hundred-dollar fine for each violation. Suppose further that the cost to the pollutor of avoiding discharge of this pollution is fifty dollars. With a 100 per cent effective enforcement mechanism, every discharge would cost one hundred dollars, and the pollutor would be induced to reduce his emissions, since by doing so he would save fifty dollars per violation over the cost of the fine. On the other hand, if only 5 per cent of all who violate the Act are caught and convicted, then the expected cost of any particular violation is no longer one hundred dollars, but one hundred dollars times 5 per cent, or five dollars. Now the pollutor must balance a five-dollar risk against a fifty-dollar expenditure to prevent the pollution. If he is not affected by some higher moral ethics, he will clearly elect not to control emissions and to pay the occasional fine when caught. The lower the probability of conviction, the higher the penalty must be in order to secure compliance.[15] Over a broad range of crimes, the percentage for which someone is actually convicted and

14 For analyses of criminal activity and penal systems in an economic framework, see
   Becker, 'Crime and Punishment: an Economic Approach,' (1968), 76 J. Pol. Econ. 169,
   and Stigler, 'The Optimum Enforcement of Laws,' (1970), 78 J. Pol. Econ. 526.
15 Becker, supra note 14, at 177

punished is very low, which has serious implications for appropriate levels of punishment.

But perhaps this model is too simple. If the pollutor persisted in violating, an injunction might be obtained specifically forbidding further violation. If this injunction were not complied with, he would be guilty not only of a violation but of contempt of court, which might raise the possibility of much higher fines. Even in such a case, every pollutor would have an incentive not to comply with the law until he had been caught and convicted and issued with an injunction. There would be no private economic reason to comply before this time.

If penalties were increased to account for a low probability of conviction, a conflict would arise between equity or justice and the effective enforcement of the law. Justice requires that the penalty be in some way proportional to the crime committed. If we interpret this as meaning that the fine should be approximately equal to the damage which might be caused by the pollution, and if the probability of conviction is small, the fine will never be sufficient to prevent the observed damage. If the fine is raised until the cost of non-compliance is approximately equal to the damage being avoided, then the 5 per cent of pollutors who are caught and convicted will be paying fines twenty times as large as the damage caused by the act which led to their conviction. Even if the law authorizes such fines, the court will hesitate to impose them. The only way out of this dilemma is to have a high prosecution and conviction rate, so that the expected cost of a violation is approximately equal to the average fine levied. In environmental problems, however, this would require a degree of surveillance far beyond the budget of any existing pollution control agency. The cost of continuously measuring emissions accurately enough to secure convictions is often almost prohibitive.[16]

One might argue that if penalties included not only fines but also possible jail sentences the deterrent would be substantially greater. The same principle, however, would still apply: the jail term should not be disproportionate to the offence if justice is to be served, and yet a low probability of conviction will mean that there is little deterrent effect. And while the

16 For an analysis of information costs and environmental policy, see Dewees *Costly Information and the Choice of Policies for Reducing Externalities* (July 1973), University of Toronto, Institute of Environmental Sciences and Engineering Publication No. EF-10. Because of the cost of precise emissions data, many air pollution laws utilize the Ringlemann Chart (referred to in Ontario as the Ontario Smoke Density Chart) which an inspector standing on the ground can compare to the colour of emissions from a smokestack to determine opacity. This is not very precise but extremely inexpensive.

disinclination of middle-class executives to become known in their community as criminals who have served time may make jail sentences particularly effective against them, the courts are frequently reluctant to send to jail those who do not appear to be in the classic mould of the hardened criminal. The jail sentences imposed in the electrical cases had a profound effect on upper management in the companies involved, but this effect was because penalties had previously been unheard of and unthinkable, not because they were severe. And anti-trust cases give us few other examples of actual jailing of corporate officers.

The same principles apply to civil litigation as to criminal prosecution. I referred earlier to the lack of incentive for the individual pollutee to sue when many persons suffer from the damage and his own injury is small. If only a small percentage of those affected do bring suit, the incentive to clean up is not great. The provision for treble damages in US anti-trust law is an attempt to correct such a situation, so that even if only one third of all those injured were to bring suit, the total cost to the pollutor would be the same as if all had brought a single damage suit. Thus, if civil actions are to be relied upon as a significant enforcement method, multiple damages may be desirable.

Decisions rendered in past prosecutions do not give hope for great optimism that the penalties imposed in particular cases will be well designed to prevent similar violations by other parties in the future. In the case of R v Eddy Match Co. Ltd,[17] Judge Bienvenue found the defendants guilty of creating a combine as defined in the Combines Investigation Act. He noted that the amount paid to shareholders by the defendant during the twenty-year period of violation was greater than $10 million, some portion of which must have been attributable to the monopoly position of the firm. However, he imposed fines totalling only $85,000, less than 10 per cent of one year's dividends paid to shareholders and probably only a small fraction of the excess profits gained by the firm over twenty years as a result of its monopoly position. No attempt was made to relate the monopoly profits reaped to the magnitude of the fine, and the court does not seem to have considered whether the fines it levied would have been sufficient to deter similar action in the future. The figures noted above suggest that the deterrent effect must have been minimal.

In the case of R v McGavin Bakeries Ltd[18] the judge at least noted that the maximum penalty that could be imposed on a corporation by law was

17 (1951) 104 C.C.C. 39, aff'd on appeal (1953) 109 C.C.C. 1
18 [1952] 1 D.L.R. 201

ten thousand dollars, which was quite inadequate under the circumstances.[19] The court did not specify the magnitude of the harm done or relate it to an appropriate penalty, although price and profit data could have suggested some order of magnitude of the gains. The court noted that the Act provided for imprisonment as well as fines, but the sentence did not include such imprisonment. This reinforces the suggestion that even where monetary sanctions are recognized as totally inadequate, courts are quite reluctant to incarcerate corporate officials for economic crimes.

American courts have at times done no better. In *American Tobacco Company* v *United States*,[20] each petitioner was fined five thousand dollars on each of three counts for a total of $255,000 in fines. The three major corporate defendants had spent $40 million per year for advertising over the several years in question, and net profits in a single year in the depths of the depression were more than $100 million. The relative magnitude of these sums should reduce any surprise that behaviour of the three firms did not substantially change after their conviction.[21]

In all of these cases, some economic analysis would have enabled the court to determine penalties more likely to deter future illegal activity. First, it is necessary to determine the excess profits earned as a result of the illegal activity. This might be measured by price increases at the time the agreement becomes effective or by differences in profit rates between firms that are party to the agreement and other firms which do not benefit. The fines imposed should be at least as great as the total excess profits actually earned. Even this, however, would only discourage future violations if there were a 100 per cent chance of being caught. If the probability of being caught is substantially less than 100 per cent for every violator, the fine must be significantly greater than the excess profits actually gained through the illegal activity.

A somewhat different problem is presented by the case of *R* v *Canadian Breweries Ltd*,[22] in which the defendant was acquitted of monopolization through merger. Despite the defendant's market share increase in Ontario from 11 to 61 per cent during the period in question, the court noted that the public was protected from monopolistic exploitation by provincial regulation of beer prices. The court failed to note that this regulation sometimes

19 Some remedy for this problem was proposed in Bill C-256, supra note 6, which provided maximum fines of one or two million dollars for most combines offences, and ten thousand dollars plus one thousand dollars per day for failure to register a merger.
20 (1946) 328 U.S. 781
21 Scherer *Industrial Market Structure and Economic Performance* (1970), at 445
22 (1960) 33 C.R. 1

consisted only of setting the retail markup, leaving the breweries free to collude in setting a monopolistic or oligopolistic wholesale price. In Ontario the legislative authority for regulation by the LCBO of retail prices is uncertain, and the history of that regulation suggests that it imposes the mildest restraint on the brewery's choice of a profit-maximizing retail price.[23] Thus, what the court interpreted as government protection of the consumer was in fact no protection at all, but rather, to some degree, government support of a cartel. Here the failure is not in sentencing but in understanding the economic forces at work in the situation. If the prices are reasonable, it is not because of regulation but because of other economic forces. Without examining prices or profits, the court could not know whether the consumer was protected or exploited.

ENFORCEMENT METHODS AND SOCIAL OBJECTIVES

In both the legislative and judicial arenas, just as for other public policy areas, including anti-combines, it is necessary to define a proper objective for environmental protection. In some environmental law suits the remedy requested has been absolute prohibition of the activity. This follows the precedent in many criminal matters where the act prohibited is *malum in se* and is therefore not permitted at all.

There may be some categories of environmental pollution which reasonably fall in this category, such as the emission of highly toxic materials. In most cases, however, environmental degradation is, or should be, *malum prohibitum*, an activity permissible to a limited extent. Some forms of pollution cannot be entirely eliminated without termination of activities which most people would agree were indispensable, such as burning of fuels or discharge of human waste. If the process must be permitted to some degree, then the question before the court or legislature is not prohibition but determining the appropriate level of limitation. Thus, while environmentalists demanded that DDT be banned because of its ill effects, it soon became apparent that in many cases the ill effects were far outweighed by the tremendous protection DDT provided for important crops. The appropriate remedy was not absolute prohibition but strict regulation and a reduction in total use.[24]

In the case of pollutants which are not immediately toxic but whose ill effects are aesthetic, or only in the long run affect human health, it seems

23 Jones, 'Mergers and Competition: The Brewing Case,' (1967), 33 *C.J.E.P.S.* 551
24 See Yannacone, supra note 13, at 337.

unreasonable to legislate that emission of a specified quantity is permissible while any more is absolutely prohibited. The difference between emitting one hundred tons or one hundred and one tons per day of particulates into the atmosphere is not in itself a matter of life or death, but a small difference in degree. This is recognized by the Ontario Air Pollution Regulations, which specify that smoke may not be darker than a certain density except for three minutes in every half hour, when it may be somewhat darker to allow for natural variation in the process producing the smoke.[25]

If the courts are to be effective in enforcing pollution control laws, they must tailor the penalties imposed to the degree of the violations. It must be clear that one who exceeds some standard only by a small amount and for a short period of time will pay a smaller fine than one who exceeds it regularly or by a large margin. In short, the penalty must be reasonably related to the harm caused by the violation, with some regard for the probability of detecting the violation. Our experience in anti-combines enforcement, however, does not provide a basis for optimism that under existing legislation courts will be able to mete out penalties that are both reasonable and effective.

The fault lies partly with existing legislation. We expect too much of a court if we enact a law which says certain acts are unlawful and may be punished by a fine of not less than two hundred and not more than ten thousand dollars. No court will have the technical expertise to determine what fine would be effective to reduce the violation, nor could it determine the relationship between the fine and the probable harm caused. And it is well known that in similar cases different judges may impose widely varying sentences.

The Ontario Environmental Protection Act shows that recent legislation offers little more guidance than in the past on the method of calculating fines for violations. Penalties are scattered throughout the act but typical are section 23(4), 'Every person who contravenes any provision of this section is guilty of an offence and on summary conviction is liable to a fine of not more than $500,'[26] and section 102(1), 'Every person ... who contravenes any provision of this Act or the regulations or fails to comply with an order ... is guilty of an offence and on summary conviction is liable on a first conviction to a fine of not more than $5,000 and on each subsequent conviction to a fine of not more than $10,000 for every day or part thereof upon which such offence occurs or continues.'[27]

25 R.R.O. 1970, Reg. 15, s. 7 (made under the Air Pollution Control Act, R.S.O. 1970, c 16)
26 The Environmental Protection Act 1971, supra note 1, s. 23(4)
27 Ibid, s. 102(1)

Section 23(4) provides a fixed fine for any offence. Section 102(1), on the other hand, provides a fine which increases after the first offence and is levied on every day of the offence. The latter is superior to the former in that it distinguishes between perpetual violators and someone who causes single or very infrequent emissions. Since the harm done by the former is greater than the latter, it seems reasonable that the penalty should correspond. Still, the law does not distinguish between the owner of a backyard incinerator and the operator of a giant steel mill. While the total emissions from two such disparate sources may be tremendous, the permissible fines are identical. Nor does the law distinguish between a neighbourhood garage disconnecting a single automotive air pollution device and an auto manufacturer producing five hundred non-complying vehicles every day. Where it is possible to define classes of violation which are more serious than others, cause greater harm, and provide greater incentives to violate the law, it is essential to provide distinctive penalties commensurate with both the harm done and the incentive to violate.

Some contrast is provided by the US automobile pollution control laws, which specify a fine of up to ten thousand dollars per violation and make every vehicle or engine not complying with the regulations count as a separate violation.[28] This provision at least provides penalties proportional to the numerical extent of the violation. However, a ten thousand-dollar fine per vehicle is clearly prohibitive since it is far above the price of most new cars. To be effective, the legislation should say something about how a court should decide the actual magnitude of the fine per vehicle. Ideally, this decision should be based on the degree to which the non-complying vehicle exceeds the standard. A car that is 2 per cent over the standard would merit a small fine, while one that is twice or three times the standard would merit much more severe penalties. The law might also provide a court some guidance as to whether the ten thousand dollars is intended to be an upper limit or a strict prohibitive fine. In short, is the penalty large because it is expected that only a small percentage of all violations will be observed, or because the harm done by any excess emission, no matter how small, causes such enormous damage that it must be prohibited under all circumstances?[29]

This raises an important distinction between most environmental laws

28 42 U.S. C.A. 1857 f-4
29 A more flexible approach to auto pollution control, in which payment is proportional to the excess of emissions over the standard, is proposed in Dewees *Economics and Public Policy: The Automobile Pollution Case* (1974) chap. 8.

and other regulations such as anti-combines laws. Under the latter, if a firm is caught in a violation, investigators can generally examine the records of that firm and others to reconstruct all violations of a similar nature which have occurred over a substantial period of time. Thus, being caught for a single current violation may lead to conviction on many past violations. To enforce environmental laws, however, actual emissions must be recorded, and it is rare for a corporation to keep such records. Thus if a pollutor is caught in one air pollution violation, this will not usually lead to conviction for previous violations. Every day of violation not directly observed by enforcement authorities must be forgotten because no proof of violation remains. This increases the importance of considering the probability that violations will lead to conviction when setting the level of punishment for non-compliance with environmental laws.

SUGGESTED REFORMS

Historically, there has been a great temptation, where complex technical and economic issues arise, to take the matter entirely out of the hands of the courts by creating an administrative agency or tribunal to set standards and enforce them.[30] Whatever the merits of such proposals for pollution control, an intermediate step which would avoid creating a new bureaucracy and preserve a more functional role for the courts would be a more explicit specification in the law itself of the kinds of penalties to be imposed in different situations.

For example, a law could specify that no emission shall be made beyond x tons per day from each plant or for each unit of final product. The law would further specify the penalty for violation as a function of the type of pollutant and the amount and frequency of the excess, so that payment of a fine is proportional to the emissions. Thus it might be specified that the standard is one hundred tons per day and ten dollars per ton must be paid for every ton in excess of that amount.

A more substantial reform could require that all pollutors record their own emissions of each specified pollutant. They would be required to pay on a regular basis for any amounts discharged in excess of existing standards according to a standard fee schedule. Payment for pollution would then become very similar to payment of taxes: regular payments without the necessity for court action and conviction. In fact, it has been suggested

30 A recent Canadian example is the Competitive Practices Tribunal proposed in Bill C-256, supra note 6.

that under such a system a profession of Certified Public Engineers analogous to Certified Accountants might arise whose job it would be to audit the companies' pollution books and certify that the records accurately indicated the amounts discharged.[31] The company and the auditor would be liable for any misrepresentations just as they are for misrepresentations in their tax and financial statements. The courts would become involved only in cases where the facts or the interpretation of the law were in dispute, rather than in every case.

There is a parallel between this kind of suggestion and existing forms of regulation. When natural monopolies occur, such as in the transportation and communications fields, the public is protected from monopoly pricing by regulatory commissions whose authority is to see that the firms earn no more than a fair rate of return on the rate base. Prices are regarded not as evil per se but as a necessary element in the firm's survival, and the prohibition of high prices is a matter of degree. If in some year the firm should earn a rate of return significantly above that allowed by the regulatory agency there is no need for court proceedings, fines, or jails. The prices are simply adjusted so that in future periods subnormal profits are earned until the excess is absorbed, or rebates may be paid to customers for the prosperous period. Here it is recognized that the difference between a good price and a bad price is not a single sharp dividing line but a continuum; the regulatory form reflects this.

A similar institutional arrangement could be imagined for pollution control. Instead of specifying all rates in the legislation, a pollution control authority would be established. Its mandate would be to ensure that total pollution emissions in a particular area do not exceed specified levels. It might issue regulations limiting emissions from each source, or it could simply specify total emissions for the area and sell the right to use some of those emissions. In either case the consequence of a firm discharging more than had been planned on or agreed to or specified would not be court action but simple payment of a sum to the pollution control authority for the excess. If the sum was reasonably related to the potential damage done or to the cost of reducing it, such a scheme could be used to ensure continual reductions in total pollution load without imposing excessive costs on any single source. It would also ensure equitable treatment among sources, unlike the present system under which some may have to impose stringent controls while others are not touched.

Any of the systems just suggested would not necessarily eliminate

31 Dales *Pollution, Property and Prices* (1968)

courts from the environmental area. Judicial resolution of conflicts arising within the administrative process will still be necessary. In addition, as previously pointed out, the history of regulation suggests that the zeal with which a new commission attacks its job may diminish over time as continued contacts build friendly relations between the regulatory body and the regulated agency. The danger will always exist that the agency would come to protect the regulated as much as it controlled them.

Because of this danger it is essential that the right of private suit be preserved. While individual litigation has proved not to be terribly effective in bringing about general improvements in environmental quality, it may still be a useful last line of defence when regulations break down. It can still protect the individual whose damage is sufficiently large to make a private action worthwhile. And in cases where only a few parties are involved and causation does not present an overwhelming problem, private litigation might be quite useful.

CONCLUSIONS

In anti-trust and anti-combines litigation, the courts have not demonstrated facility in dealing with complex economic issues, understanding the economic consequences of particular institutional arrangements, and relating penalties in individual cases to incentives for compliance with the law in the future. The result has been demands for further legislation, larger penalties, or administrative bodies and tribunals consisting largely of experts to examine most cases and dispose of them according to the legislative objectives and their particular expertise.

Environmental litigation seems to pose many of the same problems. Current legislation specifies very small fines, occasional very large fines, and no sound means of deciding what proportion of the upper limit should be imposed in a particular case. While some proposed solutions are similar, others could bring substantial improvement without necessarily moving power from the courts to administrative agencies. One solution is to design legislation which specifically relates penalties for violation to the degree of harm caused, specifying explicit schedules for certain kinds of activity so that industry can make reasonable plans to comply with the legislation. Experience has shown that very strict controls, coupled with potentially enormous fines, are as bad as no control at all since they cannot be imposed. Reasonable controls combined with penalties proportional to the harm done can, however, be quite effective.

The other improvement is to establish monitoring and surveillance systems so that a significant proportion of all offences are detected and prosecuted. This should be far easier for environmental laws than for anti-combines because of the possibility of setting standards which can be easily tested for compliance.

There are those who complain about the evils of big business in regard to both competitive behaviour and environmental degradation. On the whole, however, the evils we perceive arise not so much from evil intent on the part of large corporations as from the failure of our institutions to recognize the probable behaviour of the free enterprise system and to modify that system accordingly. Legislation that reasonably reflects the problem to be solved and the behaviour of those associated with it should enable us to achieve the desired performance, with courts playing an important but more appropriate role in the solution.

DONALD DEWEES is an associate professor of economics and an associate of the Institute for Environmental Studies, with a cross-appointment to the Faculty of Law, University of Toronto. He received his PH D in economics from Harvard, having first received an LL B from the Harvard Law School. He has written numerous articles on transportation and pollution, and his book *Economics and Public Policy: The Automobile Pollution Case* has recently been published by the MIT Press.

KENNETH McNAUGHT

Political trials and the Canadian political tradition

An American scholar, T. Becker, wrote recently that 'in a sense, all trials are political. Since courts are governmental agencies and judges are part of the "system" all judicial decisions can be considered political.'[1] This excessively commodious definition is less useful than one proffered by Professor Nathan Hakman when he suggests that courtroom participants act politically when their activities involve other members of society. Hakman then proposes that scholars can conceptualize conscious or unconscious use of court cases as '(1) an instrument for securing private and personal remedies; or (2) an instrument for changing legal symbols (i.e., applicable rules of law); or (3) a means of organizing and/or suppressing movements for social and economic power and control.'[2] Even this approach to a definition casts a very wide net. Within it one could catch hundreds of 'test cases' – from *Roncarelli* to the Bennett New Deal legislation.

I suspect that a Canadian attempt to define a political trial would result in more constrictive language. We have never been as ready as the Americans, for example, to view the courts as means for changing 'legal symbols' – especially if such a process includes implementing significant social

1 Becker *Political Trials* (1971)
2 Hakman, 'Political Trials in the Legal Order: A Political Scientist's Perspective,' (1972), 21 *J. Public Law* 73 at 81

This article is a slightly revised version of one which appeared in (1974), 24 *UTLJ* 149.

change. Thus, under Hakman's third rubric, our courts have seldom, if ever, been used to 'organize movements for social and economic power and control'; they have, however, very often been used in attempts to suppress such movements. It may very well be because of this Canadian tradition that attempts to politicize some recent trials – such as the FLQ cases, the Quebec labour leaders' trial, and the lesser cases of student anti-war and 'occupation' demonstrators – seem largely to have failed, at least by comparison with the Angela Davis case, the Black Panther cases, the Ellsburg case, or the Chicago trials in Judge Hoffman's court.

A preliminary survey of Canadian political trials strongly suggests that our judges and lawyers, supported by the press and public opinion, reject any concept of the courts as positive instruments in the political process. In Canada the positive aspects of politics seem more clearly to belong to the political parties, the legislatures, and the press. A corollary of this is that political action outside the party-parliamentary structure tends automatically to be suspect – and not least because it smacks of Americanism. This deep-grained Canadian attitude of distinguishing amongst proper and improper methods of dealing with societal organization and problems reveals us as being, to some extent, what Walter Bagehot once called a 'deferential society.' We have certainly shown deference to the concept of *established* authority and procedures and even to the legal idea that valid authority flows downward from the crown.

Far from being merely medieval, such attitudes have often proven more liberal in their effect than those of radical or participatory democracy. In any event, the basically British belief that both liberty and justice are impossible without order lies at the heart of the Canadian political tradition and of the manner in which our judicial process has dealt with cases of a clearly political nature. Since it is within the context of that tradition that the courts have acted (while helping to enforce and expound it) let me suggest by a very few quotations how widely the tradition has been endorsed.

It is appropriate to begin with John Beverley Robinson CJUC who, in sentencing Samuel Lount and Peter Matthews to be hanged for their part in the 1837 rebellion, recalled to them the Christian and civil duties they had forsworn. Not only had it been their 'bounden duty' to support the constitution, Robinson admonished them, they had not been sufficiently perspicacious to understand the benefits of holding 'that middle station of life than which none is happier; you were your own masters ... Higher rank and greater wealth might have enabled you to live with less actual labour of your hands; but it is not certain that they would have increased your enjoyment. On the contrary, they often bring with them care and anxiety, while they attract jealousy and envy.'[3] A perfect Tory statement of the blessings of a structured society – to which we will return later; and to which it is proper to append certain remarks of William Lyon Mackenzie who was not hanged in 1837 only because he was not caught in arms. After living in the United States and working for such renowned democrats as Horace Greeley of the *New York Tribune*, in 1849 Mackenzie availed himself of a general amnesty to return to Canada. He immediately wrote thus to the British colonial secretary, Earl Grey: 'A course of careful observation during the last eleven years has fully satisfied me that had the violent movements in which I and others were engaged on both sides of the Niagara proved successful, that success would have deeply injured the people of Canada, whom I then believed I was serving at great risks ... No punishment that power could inflict, or nature sustain, would have equalled the regrets I have felt on account of much that I did, said, wrote and published ... There is not a living man on this continent who more sincerely desires that British government in Canada may long continue.'[4] Indeed, when one considers the aftermath of political crises and trials in Canada, from Mackenzie and Papineau, to some of the spies unmasked by Igor Gouzenko, and on to Pierre Vallières, one might conclude that few countries have witnessed the repentance of such a high proportion of political rebels. It is not impossible that a major reason for this has been the combination of firm action and succeeding lenience which seems to characterize our basically conservative political-judicial tradition. It seems unlikely, for example, that had Vallières been as closely implicated in a revolutionary movement in the American republican democracy as he was in Quebec he would today not only be free but the beneficiary of a federal grant to assist community organization.

Conversely to the conventional wisdom of Canadian history, it may well be that our judicial history indicates that we have had somewhat more confidence in the validity of our institutions and our whole national experiment than have the Americans in theirs.[5] Sir John A. Macdonald, with his

---

3 *Address of the Honourable Chief Justice Robinson, on passing sentence of death upon Samuel Lount and Peter Matthews* (1838), Library of the Law Society of Upper Canada
4 Reprinted in 2 Dent *The Story of the Upper Canadian Rebellion* (1885), at 306
5 The question of Canadian 'lack of identity' as opposed to self-confident American republican democracy is increasingly interesting. Canadians are *taught* to feel insecure, whereas in fact they are far more secure than their American counterparts. It is very unlikely that an American president could have invoked a War Measures Act, had one existed, in American circumstances roughly comparable to those of 1970 in this country. In fact a major

talent for compression, summed up the purpose and the self-confidence of the Canadian experiment when he remarked during the 1864 Quebec Conference: 'Thus we shall have a strong and lasting government under which we can work out constitutional liberty as opposed to democracy, and be able to protect the minority by having a strong central government.'[6] Constitutional liberty has remained the other side of the Canadian monarchical coin. When J.S. Woodsworth, in September 1939, rose as the only member of the House of Commons to record his vote against the Canadian declaration of war he remarked, 'I have boys of my own, and I hope they are not cowards, but if any one of those boys, not from cowardice but really through belief, is willing to take his stand on this matter and, if necessary, to face a concentration camp or a firing squad, I shall be more proud of that boy than if he enlisted for war.'[7] This was technically seditious, especially since Woodsworth repeated the sentiments outside the House, and very similar to the remarks which sent the American socialist Eugene Debs to jail in 1918 on a twenty-year sentence. Although the War Measures Act had not yet been proclaimed the prime minister had already referred to 'the enemy,' and by constitutional precedent Canada was at war immediately upon the British declaration of 3 September.[8] Thus, toward the end of his speech Woodsworth said 'I rejoice that it is possible to say these things in a Canadian Parliament under British institutions. It would not be possible in Germany, I recognize that ... and I want to maintain the very essence of our British institutions of real liberty. I believe that the only way to do it is by an

---

explanation of American political behaviour is the *absence* of self-assuredness. As Professor C. Vann Woodward has put it: 'Lacking a common racial, religious, linguistic, or political heritage, they had to look elsewhere for the bases of nationality. Their anxiety over this quest for national identity helps explain ... "a somewhat compulsive preoccupation with the question of their Americanism." ' Woodward *The Comparative Approach to American History* (1968), at 6

6 Pope *Confederation Documents* (1895), at 54. In the Confederation Debates of 1865 Sir G.-E. Cartier underlined the widespread acceptance of continuity and legitimacy: 'In our federation the monarchical principle would form the leading feature, while on the other side of the line ... the ruling power was the will of the mob ... and mob rule had consequently supplanted legitimate authority.'

7 House of Commons *Debates* (1939 Special Session), at 41

8 For further discussion of these points see McNaught, 'Canadian Foreign Policy and the Whig Interpretation: 1936–1939,' (1957), Can. Hist. Assoc. *Report*, and *A Prophet in Politics* (1959), chap. 20. Woodsworth was, of course, well aware of his position, having been fired by the Manitoba government in 1917 for opposing national registration and being still technically under a 1919 indictment for seditious libel, upon which a *nolle prosequi* had been entered.

appeal to the moral forces still resident among our people, and not by another resort to brute force.'

For the purpose of hypothesizing the relation of our courts to this kind of political tradition I propose a very narrow definition of 'political trial,' that is, one in which there appears to be an overt confrontation between the principles or forces of social change and those of social and/or constitutional continuity. Canadian courts dealing with such cases often reveal to the historian the most basic political assumptions of our society, the nature and limits of political tolerance, change, and/or continuity in the social-economic basis of the country, and how political trials can occasionally bring to a head significant issues of press freedom, religious freedom, and the relation of both to established political authority. On the basis of this definition I propose to discuss a number of trials or cases scattered from 1814 to the present. Some involve confrontation between essentially internal forces of continuity and of change; some directly implicate foreign sources of support for changes in the Canadian condition;[9] and two involve freedom of the press in political discussion.

LOUNT AND MATTHEWS

The first group is the most important, although one cannot help but be impressed by how much is revealed in less prominent cases. In 1838, when Lount and Matthews were tried before Chief Justice Robinson on the charge of treason for their parts in the Mackenzie rebellion, the situation was both volatile and complex. On the one hand both of the accused pleaded guilty. On the other, the province was still in turmoil. The jails were jammed with captured rebels, and many reformers were considering emigrating to the United States – partly because of anticipated repression, partly because of the continuing depression which had been a major cause of the rebellion. It was in these circumstances that Robinson sentenced the two men to death. In so doing he revealed a supreme confidence in the rightness both of the legal and the political system of Upper Canada. As suggested above he also took the occasion to expound the social-political

9 Of course a large number of our political trials, even apart from those which have overt foreign connotations, have had more or less foreign implications. The 1837 rebels proposed an American solution to Canadian problems and both hoped for and helped organize American intervention; in 1885 Riel was an American citizen and sought intervention by the State Department to prevent his being tried for treason; Tim Buck was clearly working under direction of the Comintern; the FLQ had direct connections, tactical and ideological, with Algeria, the Palestinian liberationists, and Cuba.

principles of the community, as he saw them.[10] Those principles were essentially Lockean, but they had a strong Tory touch.[11] 'You were not' he reminded the condemned men 'the tenants of rigorous and exacting landlords; you were not burthened with taxes for the State, further than the payment perhaps of a few shillings in the year, to support the common expenses of the District in which you lived ... Regularity and industry would always have ensured you a competency.' Robinson went on to underline the relation of liberty to authority: 'You lived in a country where every man who obeys the laws is secure in the protection of life, liberty, and property;[12] under a form of government, which has been the admiration of the world for ages.' After telling the prisoners that they could easily, and without reproach, have sold their possessions and moved to the United States (had they preferred a republic to a monarchy) the chief justice spelled out the Tory side of his discourse: 'There is no doubt the chief cause [of your dreadful fall] has been your wilful forgetfulness of your duty to your Creator, and of the purposes for which life was bestowed upon you ... You have, I fear, too long and unreservedly indulged in a feeling of envy and hatred towards your rulers – which was sure to undermine every just and generous sentiment, and to lead in the end to the ruin of your happiness and peace.'[13] To Lount, who had been a member of the Legislative Assembly, Robinson was particularly stringent: 'In a country in which you have been admitted to the honourable privilege of making laws to bind your fellow subjects, it was due from *you* to set an example of faithful obedience to public authority ... as a man, as a subject, and as a Christian.' The chief justice then said that he could hold out no hope of pardon and implored the condemned men to 'address yourselves in humble and earnest sincerity to the infinite mercy of that Saviour whose divine commands you have transgressed.'

10 Supra note 3
11 For an illuminating discussion of the 'Tory touch' in an otherwise Lockean society see Horowitz *Canadian Labour in Politics* (1968), chap. 1.
12 It is interesting that Robinson took his phrase directly from Locke rather than from Jefferson who changed 'property' to 'pursuit of happiness.'
13 Robinson at this point expressed an undiluted Tory view on a partially extraneous matter: 'It is one of the miserable consequences of the abuse of liberty, that a licentious press is permitted to poison the public mind with the most absurd and wicked misrepresentations which the ill-disposed, without inquiry, receive and act upon as truths. It is, to be sure, in the power of the laws to restrain this evil to a certain extent, or, at least, they may attempt to do so; but such is the perverseness of a great portion of mankind, that whenever it is endeavoured to exert this power, the attempt is felt, and resented, as an infringement upon liberty.'

Sentence was carried out on 12 April 1838, but not before the Executive Council of Upper Canada had reconsidered it in the light of petitions bearing eight thousand signatures. In a report to the Colonial Office[14] the new governor, Sir George Arthur, observed that the chief justice, the attorney general, and the entire council agreed, despite previous instructions from London that 'circumspection' was requisite 'in carrying into effect any capital sentences passed upon persons convicted of political offences,' that it could not recommend interfering with the course of justice. The cases in question, reported Arthur, 'are of the greatest emergency ... severe public example is actually required in some cases.' As 'leaders and instigators' Lount and Matthews were 'particularly fit to be selected for capital punishment.'

One of the reasons, perhaps, that Robinson took such pains with his address in 1838 was that he was virtually certain the sentence would stand without appeal or executive reversal. He knew that his statements would take on an added importance because he was presiding over what was in reality a supreme court. It may be that a decline in the calibre of such judicial statements over the following century is related to the development of an extensive superstructure of federal and imperial appeal courts.[15] Certainly this case sheds a good deal of light on the social-political assumptions of Upper Canada, especially when taken in conjunction with the leniency shown to the other incarcerated rebels. The final general amnesty of 1849, together with the Rebellion Losses legislation, suggests a society which felt secure enough in its basic attitudes toward legitimacy to act quickly when those attitudes were challenged while showing extreme leniency once the threat appeared to have passed.

LOUIS RIEL

Forty-seven years after the executions of 1838 Louis Riel dropped through the scaffold at Regina. His is by far the most complicated political trial from

14 Public Archives of Canada, Q Series, Arthur to Glenelg, 14 April 1938. This long dispatch contains an excellent summary of the trial's aftermath.
15 Robinson also had the advantage of being on very close terms with Governor Arthur and could thus anticipate the remarks sent by the governor to the Colonial Office immediately following the executions: 'when your Lordship shall have read the proceedings of the Council, I trust you will be convinced that I ought not, from any apprehension of responsibility, to have respited these convicts for the purpose of sending their cases to England, as no recommendation for mercy could possibly accompany them.' Ibid. A comparison of Robinson's address with the judgment delivered by Mulock, CJO in *R. v Buck*, [1932] 3 D.L.R. 97 (Ont. C.A.) is depressing.

a historian's point of view. To lawyers it is unique for two reasons: first, Riel is the only citizen of a foreign state to have been tried for treason in Canada,[16] and second, he is the only person in Canadian history to be hanged for treason who had himself conducted a political trial resulting in execution of the accused. To the historian Riel is unique in another respect: he led our only successful democratic rebellion.[17] However, achievement of provincial status for Manitoba in 1870 had been heavily shadowed by the execution of the Ontario Orangeman Thomas Scott. Scott was tried under 'Métis law' in an ad hoc court for 'insubordination' to Riel's provisional government, and Riel made the fatal mistake of permitting the death sentence to be carried out, exclaiming to Donald Smith who had pleaded for remission: 'We must make Canada respect us.'[18]

Although Ontario howled for Riel's blood, Macdonald allowed him to go unapprehended. Thus, when Riel was captured during his unsuccessful second rebellion there could be little doubt that, if convicted and sentenced to death, commutation would present serious political dangers. The historical significance of the trial is therefore very great indeed. It continued to focus attention on the Métis and Indian grievances by suggesting that mere suppression of the rebellion would not settle the problems created by a conflict of cultures and by governmental insouciance. Riel's own version of his defence was that the 'insane' party in the case was the government of Canada, and there were many newspapers (including the Toronto *Globe*) that agreed with him. Indeed the very organization of his legal defence, supervised by L.O. David and including Wilfrid Laurier and Rodolphe LaFlamme, reads like the establishment list of French Canadian Liberalism. The trial and execution, more than the rebellion itself, brought to a head the deepest potential conflict in Canadian society; to Quebec Riel became a figure of innocence and rejected aspirations, to Ontario a figure of political criminality. The bitterness unleashed by Macdonald's refusal to have the sentence commuted became a major factor in moving Quebec from the Conservative to the Liberal party in federal politics. However, the trial itself also raises some interesting questions.

The lawyers provided for Riel by his Quebec-based defence committee were François Lemieux, Charles Fitzpatrick, and J.N. Greenshields. None of them knew anything about the west and it remains a real question whether they helped or hindered Riel during the trial. Riel was so clearly

16 Riel became an American citizen while teaching school in Montana.
17 Whether one succeeds or fails at rebellion in Canada one receives a statue: Papineau, Mackenzie, Riel.
18 Stanley *Louis Riel* (1963), at 114

guilty of treason that the only serious question throughout was that of mitigating circumstances which might soften the eventual sentence. His lawyers, against Riel's strenuous opposition, elected to plead insanity. It seems plausible, despite a mountain of conflicting evidence as to Riel's sanity (that is, responsibility for his actions), that his own unremitting effort to *accept* responsibility is the most convincing aspect of the trial and of the lengthy post-trial period pending his execution. Riel wrote, prior to his trial: 'I desire that my trial should turn on the merits of my actions.'[19] It did not. It turned on the question of his sanity, introducing such items as his prophetic pretensions and plans to resettle the discordant populations of Europe in the New World. Riel felt that gratitude prevented him from dismissing his lawyers, as he was tempted to do when he found that they could not question the crown's witnesses in the way that he knew was essential. His lawyers, he remarked, 'come from Quebec, from a far province' and had to question men 'with whom they are not acquainted, on circumstances which they don't know.' Although Riel suggested questions, 'they cannot follow the thread of all the questions that could be put to the witnesses. They lose more than three-quarters of the good opportunities.' Judge Richardson was prepared to allow Riel to cross-question the witnesses, but his lawyers said they would withdraw if he were allowed to do so. Riel was forced to subside with the bitter cry: 'Here I have to defend myself against the accusation of high treason, or I have to consent to the animal life of an asylum.'[20] In the result he was allowed to address the jury only after his lawyers had finished. Then Riel made his essential point: 'If you take the plea of the defence that I am not responsible for my acts, acquit me completely, since I have been quarreling with an insane and irresponsible Government. If you pronounce in favour of the Crown which contends that I am responsible, acquit me all the same. You are perfectly justified in declaring that having my reason and sound mind, I have acted reasonably and in self-defence, while the Government, my accuser, being irresponsible, and consequently insane, cannot but have acted wrong.'[21]

When one considers that a six-man, English-speaking jury, after finding Riel guilty of treason, recommended him to 'the mercy of the Crown,' it is reasonable to ask whether their unadorned recommendation might not have been stronger had Riel been permitted to cross-examine the crown's witnesses. In the light of the political reactions there is little doubt about two aspects of the case. First, it confirmed the principle established in 1838

19 Ibid, at 343
20 Ibid, at 350-1
21 Ibid, at 356

that if resort is had to violence, no matter how just the cause, it must be decisively condemned; and second, if an element of racial or cultural conflict enters into a political trial either a jury or a judge is likely to find reasons for compassion. In the case of Riel the jury's recommendation of mercy was overlooked only because of the Scott affair (an exceptional circumstance) and Macdonald's assessment of the political repercussions in Ontario.[22]

WINNIPEG GENERAL STRIKE

The cases arising from the Winnipeg General Strike of 1919 also reveal racial tensions but, much more importantly, they cast a bright light on the impact of industrialization, urbanization, immigration, and the continuities of regionalism in Canada.[23]

Winnipeg had grown from 42,000 in 1901 to 200,000 in 1919, and one-third of that population was foreign-born. As railway and marketing centre of the prairie wheat economy the city had developed supportive industry, especially in the metal and building trades. It had also developed a highly structured, class-conscious society. The men of power in Winnipeg, geographically isolated yet closely intertwined with central Canadian business and political organizations, were virtually all of Ontario lineage. They belonged to what John Porter designates as the principal Canadian 'charter group,'[24] and they had no intention of loosening their control over government or economic life. Welcoming the new labour force supplied by the wheat boom immigration, these men vigorously resisted the claims of growing trade unions to recognition and bargaining rights. The buoyant business activity of first world war years had been preceded by a long period of increasingly bitter industrial strife.[25] As the war neared its end, organized labour in Winnipeg redoubled its efforts to secure full union

22 In cases where strong public emotions are aroused – such as those attaching to race or freedom of the press – it may be that the defendant is well advised to conduct his own courtroom defence. Joseph Howe (Halifax, 1835) and Fred Dixon (Winnipeg, 1920) each defended himself successfully against substantial charges of politically libellous publication.

23 Accounts of the strike may be found in Masters *The Winnipeg General Strike* (1950), Robin *Radical Politics and Canadian Labour* (1968), McNaught *A Prophet in Politics* (1959), and McNaught and Bercuson *The Winnipeg Strike: 1919* (1974). The 'racial tensions,' of course, were not French-English but those which stemmed from the post-1896 immigration from east-central Europe.

24 Porter *The Vertical Mosaic* (1965), especially at 60ff

25 For analysis of these years see Bercuson *Confrontation at Winnipeg* (1974).

recognition, anticipating serious unemployment with the return of the soldiers, while a rapidly rising cost of living sharpened concerns for the future. Undoubtedly, too, the Russian revolution, together with world-wide interest in the *method* of the general strike as the most effective way to achieve economic gains, industrial (as opposed to craft) unionism, and/or basic social change, further induced radical labour action in Winnipeg. As is evident in court cases following the strike (the largest and most nearly successful general strike in North America) the courts spoke not only for the Winnipeg establishment but also for the entire Canadian bourgeoisie as well as for most farmers.

In these cases, from the preliminary hearings through to the appeal judgments, an interpretation of the strike was promulgated which was an *esquisse* of the arguments put forth by the strike's opponents. The problem for the legal historian is to understand the relation between what 'actually happened,' the interpretation of what happened used by the courts in their judgments, and the legal-political function of the judgments as precedents.[26]

What 'actually happened' began on 15 May when a general strike vote conducted by the Winnipeg Trades and Labour Council went into effect with the declared purpose of achieving industrial union recognition and wage raises in the building and metal trades – whose unions were already on strike. Thirty-five thousand workers left their jobs,[27] including those who operated all the public utilities, and the economic life of the city remained at a standstill for six weeks. Fearing forcible suppression, the strike leaders managed to keep the immensely volatile situation almost completely non-violent. Yet the massive show of economic strength, together with the fact that a majority of the returned soldiers seemed sympathetic to the strikers, induced a condition close to hysteria in the 'middle class' of Winnipeg, a class heavily influenced by lurid reports of the great Red Scare in the United States. Yet, while opposition to such a dramatic assertion of working-class demands was bound to be vigorous, the structural and ideological unity of that opposition was even more startling than

26 The Robson Report (*Report of the Royal Commission to Enquire into and Report upon the Causes and Effects of the General Strike ... in the City of Winnipeg ... H.A. Robson, K.C., Commissioner, Winnipeg, 1919*), together with all the more recent studies of the strike, concludes that the 'causes' were not those of a vast revolutionary conspiracy but rather the felt need for industrial unionism and higher wages to keep pace with post-war inflation.

27 Only twelve thousand of the strikers were union members, and this clear intimation of the *political* strength of the working class was a major reason for the politicization of the strike and the trials by business-legal leaders.

the original cohesion of the working class. In a very real sense the strike's opponents planned their course of action and their frequent public statements as preparation for the ultimate resort to the courts. The politicization of the strike thus was the necessary foundation for the politicization of the trials. The point may be illustrated in many ways; a few examples must here suffice.

The case to be constructed was that the strike was an attempt to usurp constituted authority; that by its very nature it must become violent in order to achieve its end of establishing a soviet government in Winnipeg; and that it was principally the work of the much-feared, disloyal immigrants – those whose immediate deportation as 'alien scum' and 'bohunks' was demanded by J.W. Dafoe's *Free Press*.[28] The required violence was produced by two measures. First was the dismissal of the municipal police force (whose members had remained on duty while declaring their support of the strike) and its replacement by a force of untrained 'specials' which provoked a minor riot on 11 June. The second incident of violence grew out of two similar arbitrary actions. The first of these was the arrest of eight strike leaders and four men who had no connection with the strike committee but who were foreign-born and whose names leant plausibility to fears of an alien conspiracy.[29] This truncating of the strike leadership angered the pro-strike veterans who organized a massive 'silent parade' to demand of Senator Gideon Robertson (federal minister of labour) an explanation of the arrests. When the paraders refused to disperse the mayor read the Riot Act and a large contingent of Royal Northwest Mounted Police charged three times through the crowds, the third time shooting with revolvers. Two men were killed, and the centre of the city was occupied by heavily armed militiamen. A few days later the strike was called off.

No one can read the background of the 1919–20 trials, follow the evidence presented at those trials,[30] and miss the unbroken theme of a case-to-be-made. The federal cabinet, the district military commander, and the RNWMP commissioner worked in the closest possible liaison with the Citizens' Committee which was organized by Winnipeg lawyers and businessmen to crush the strike and assert seditious intent. Symbolic of the interlocking arrangement was A.J. Andrews, who, as a prominent lawyer, ex-mayor, business and personal friend of Arthur Meighen (acting federal

---

28 *Manitoba Free Press*, (7, 11 June 1919)

29 One of the aliens, a man named Verenchuk, was picked up accidentally while looking after a friend's house. His name did not appear on the RNWMP warrant until thirty-six hours after he entered Stony Mountain Penitentiary.

30 Particularly *R* v *Russell*, (1919), 29 M.R. 511; aff'd (1920) 33 C.C.C. 1

justice minister), and prominent in the Citizens' Committee, was appointed special agent of the department of justice, planned the arrests, and became chief crown prosecutor in the trials. While the Citizens' Committee was trying to establish that violent revolution was the real goal of the strike, government spokesmen hammered home the same point, as when Meighen declared in the Commons that it was 'essential that the greater issue raised by the assumption of Soviet authority – and it was nothing less on the part of those in control of the strike in the city of Winnipeg – should be once and for all decided and be decisively beaten down.'[31] At the last moment, after the arrests, the government hesitated about bringing the leaders to trial for sedition, and Meighen wired Andrews: 'Notwithstanding any doubt I have as to the technical legality of the arrests and the detention at Stony Mountain, I feel that rapid deportation is the best course now that the arrests are made, and later we can consider ratification.'[32] Such a course would probably have been disastrous for the government. In the event, the decision to prosecute, which was most forcefully argued by Andrews, was accepted as the logical consummation of the whole anti-strike strategy. The eight leaders, Russell, Ivens, Queen, Bray, Armstrong, Heaps, Johns, and Pritchard were charged with seditious conspiracy. Shortly after the police-military action of 21 June, J.S. Woodsworth and F.J. Dixon were arrested on charges of seditious libel for continuing to publish the strikers' newspaper and printing critical accounts of 'Bloody Saturday.'

The crown's case that the economic goals of the strike were but incidental to a socialist revolutionary conspiracy which had been allegedly hatched at Calgary in the previous April was sustained by juries composed largely of farmers. The evidence, both of conspiracy and of seditious intent, consisted of the most radical socialist statements made over the preceding months by the defendants, together with their membership in

31 House of Commons *Debates* (1919), at 3039ff. The question of how far the official case was actually believed by those who constructed it is a difficult one. Certainly Gideon Robertson and Arthur Meighen gave many indications, public and private, that the main threat was to the dominance in Canada of what Robertson called 'the sober leaders of organized labour in the United States.' In the same debate Meighen, after conceding that the country's employers were highly organized, rejected the same degree of organization as a legitimate goal of labour: 'Can any one contemplate such an event? ... Are we to have on the one hand a concentration of employers, and on the other hand a concentration of all the labour interests of the Dominion, fighting it out for supremacy?'

32 House of Commons *Debates* (1926), at 4004ff. Despite frequent references to the alien threat all the strike leaders were British-born (except one who was born in Ontario) and the government had taken the precaution, during the strike, of amending the Immigration Act to permit deportation of British subjects, who were not Canadian-born, without jury trial.

organizations which advocated replacing the capitalist political-economic system with a socialist one. Yet, despite widespread police raids on labour offices and homes across the country, no evidence of preparation for, or specific advocacy of, the use of violence was produced.[33] The verdicts and sentences[34] may thus be presumed to flow from three principal conditions: the fact that the juries were composed of farmers who, as a class, were deeply hostile to the general strike; the extraordinarily circular definition of sedition in the Criminal Code;[35] and the decision by the judges to advise the juries that the prosecution had successfully proven that 'force' had been threatened.[36]

Partly because opinion in Winnipeg was so deeply divided about the nature of the strike and its suppression, the sentences served further to politicize the situation. In the Manitoba election of 1920, Ivens, Queen, and Armstrong all won election to the legislature although they were still in jail and had stood on socialist platforms. F.J. Dixon topped the polls in Win-

33 The crown's claim that the Mounties were fired upon before drawing their own revolvers on 21 June does not stand up well against recent research; see Bercuson and McNaught, *The Winnipeg Strike: 1919* (1974). It now seems clear that the order to fire resulted from general stone-and-stick harassment of the charging police and not from any shots fired from the crowd. No weapons were found on those arrested at the scene or in the later evidence-seeking raids.

34 Of the eight strike leaders arrested, Russell received two years for seditious conspiracy; Ivens, Johns, Pritchard, Queen, and Armstrong each received one year on the same charge; Bray received six months for being a 'common nuisance'; Heaps won an acquittal. F.J. Dixon, charged with seditious libel, defended himself and was acquitted – after which the crown entered a *nolle prosequi* on the similar charge against J.S. Woodsworth.

35 For an interesting discussion of the definitional problem see Katz, 'Some legal consequences of the Winnipeg General Strike of 1919,' (1970), 4 *Manitoba L.J.* 39.

36 The propriety of this judicial comment was asserted in the Russell appeal case, especially by Cameron, JA, supra note 30, at 14–15. Despite the crown's emphasis on the 'conspirators'' disloyalty to the British form of government, Cameron underlined the differences between Canadian and British law on the rights of picketing, sympathetic strikes, secondary boycotts, etc. He further commented that 'the term "sympathetic strike" may convey the idea of workmen in certain industries ceasing work voluntarily and without breach of their own contracts to express their sympathy for and moral support of other workmen already on strike. On this continent it is certainly not confined in meaning to any such peaceful demonstration ... or to the apparently identical term "secondary strike" in England ... Here we have been educated to give the terms "general" or "sympathetic strike" much wider meanings and to so expand them as to include even the idea which underlies the significant phrase "direct action."' This pioneer continentalist then cited several American cases and quoted with approval an article commenting on them: 'If the strike is in the nature of a boycott or sympathetic strike – that is, if it involves no trade dispute between the strikers and their employer ... the strike cannot be justified and is therefore always an illegal one.'

nipeg while, in 1921, J.S. Woodsworth became the first federal MP to be elected by a social-democratic party. In declaring, very dubiously, an 'apprehended insurrection' and by applying massive state violence, the anti-strike class had politically radicalized large numbers of Winnipeg's working class. It had also given fresh arguments to those leaders who believed that political party action (parliamentarism) must be the complement of economic action. The new condition of urban industrialism had been thoroughly, if with pronounced bias, examined by the courts for its inherent political dangers. One significant outcome was the amending of the Criminal Code in 1919 to increase the permissible sentence for sedition from two to twenty years and still further to broaden the 'definition' of sedition. The revision was to prove convenient in obtaining convictions, amongst others, of J.B. McLachlan for his role in the extended industrial conflict in Nova Scotia in the early twenties and of Tim Buck for his membership in the Communist party in the thirties. As the worst of the depression passed, and with the political threat of the CCF increasingly worrisome to Mackenzie King, section 98 was finally repealed in 1937.[37]

QUEBEC 1970

If the Winnipeg trials and their aftermath illuminated the potential for state-originated violence in urban-industrial Canada, the October 1970

37 One of the best illustrations of the breadth of definition given to sedition by s. 98 is to be found in the judgment of Mulock CJO in the Buck appeal ([1932] 3 D.L.R. 97). Mulock upheld the conviction of Buck and seven colleagues on the charge that they 'did act or profess to act as officers of an unlawful association, to wit, the Communist Party of Canada.' Despite the zeal of Sgt J. Leopold (RCMP), who was a member of the Party for seven years, no direct evidence that the defendants had organized or advocated specific acts of violence had been produced in the original trial. On the basis of lengthy excerpts from reports of the Communist International Mulock agreed with the original decision that under s. 98 the Party was illegal and its officers therefore guilty of sedition. Seven received sentences totalling five years each; one, three years. The case of J.B. McLachlan shows how the definition of seditious libel was equally broadened. Secretary of District 26, United Mine Workers of America (Nova Scotia), McLachlan published an 'official' letter (4 July 1923) in several newspapers condemning police and military brutality in the mining towns where his union was on strike against a pay cut of $37^1/2$ per cent. 'The Government of Nova Scotia' wrote McLachlan 'is the guilty and responsible party for this crime.' The only conceivable 'incitement' in the letter was an exhortation to spread the strike 'to every mine in Nova Scotia.' For this seditious matter he was convicted and sentenced to two years. The judgment was confirmed on appeal, despite some learned doubts about the admissibility as evidence of certain 'radical' books found in the defendant's library. See R. v McLachlan, (1923), 56 N.S.R. 413.

crisis in Quebec exhibited the continuing dominance of the idea of legitimacy in government. However, these two cases of state 'repression' contain superficial similarities which have often seemed to obscure the profound differences in almost every aspect of comparison.[38] The most important of the apparent similarities is the assertion by government, in each case, of apprehended insurrection.[39] However, as previously observed, violence in Winnipeg had to be provoked by governmental actions; there is now a historical consensus that the policy of the strike committee was non-violent and the aims were specific improvements in the conditions and organization of the working class. In the case of Quebec it is uncontested that the declared policy of the Front de libération du Québec was that of violence and terror, that such a policy had been put into effect, and that the FLQ purpose was reconstitution of the state by non-parliamentary means. The only question still at issue is the extent to which Montreal (essentially) was inflammable. Here the evidence is both extensive and contentious. Curiously, the FLQ evidence itself is contradictory, as in the conversations of the Cross kidnappers, taped while they were awaiting capture and exile to Cuba.[40] On the one hand the terrorists felt that 'the federal cabinet was surprised, even astonished to see the popular support the manifesto received.' On the other hand, 'we were double-crossed by the federal government ... I mean the federal government stirred up the city much more than we thought they could.' Critics of the governmental response to the kidnapping argue that not enough dynamite or other weaponry was discovered by police to justify an apprehension of insurrection. But such analysis seems simply to underline the differences between the Winnipeg of 1919 and the Montreal of 1970 – differences which were further illuminated by the respective legal dispositions.

In the aftermath of the Lesage 'Quiet Revolution' a frustrated professional class became increasingly sympathetic to strident *nationaliste* demands while a long series of bombings, strike violence, and street demonstrations seemed to illustrate the vulnerability of contemporary urban society to new methods of undermining the credibility of elected gov-

38 The most objective comprehensive account of the FLQ crisis is Saywell *Quebec 70* (1971).
39 The seditious conspiracy charges in the Winnipeg cases were simply the legal synonym for the governmental and Citizens' Committee allegations of 'usurpation of constituted authority' accompanied by 'threatened violence,' and each is a synonym for 'apprehended insurrection.' And, of course, the 'Montreal Five,' Lemieux, Gagnon, Vallières, Chartrand, and Larue-Langlois, were also charged with seditious conspiracy.
40 Saywell, supra note 38, at 129ff

ernments.[41] The actual number of declared revolutionaries and calculations of firepower had little real bearing on the ability of a dedicated terrorist organization to bring about a situation in which mass disorder and fear could put an end to democratic constitutionalism.

The unpredictable element of racial nationalism in the Quebec of 1970 produced another major difference in any comparison with 1919 Winnipeg. Appeals to race and nationalism were not wanting in Winnipeg, but fear of the 'alien' threat from below was very different from Quebec *nationaliste* hatred of 'alien' domination from above. Thus in Winnipeg the state tried to politicize the crisis and the resulting trials. In 1970 the state did its best to depoliticize the criminal acts of the FLQ. While the FLQ manifesto and communiqués during the kidnapping crisis all referred to previously convicted terrorists as 'political prisoners,' both the federal and Quebec governments insisted that 'these were not political prisoners, inasmuch as they had all been condemned or were under accusation by virtue of our civil (criminal) law.'[42] Yet even while the governments involved were endeavouring to downplay the political nature of the crisis in order to minimize sympathy for those already in jail and those who would inevitably be brought to court, proclamation of the War Measures Act on 16 October, and of public order regulations under authority of the Act, underlined the political nature of the crisis.

The granting of emergency powers of search, arrest, and detention, together with retroactive operation of provisions declaring the FLQ an unlawful association, raise another point of comparison with the earlier Winnipeg crisis. In 1919 the War Measures Act was still in effect but was not employed to authorize use of special police, RNWMP and militia, mid-

---

41 Jérôme Choquette explained for the Quebec government this aspect of volatility: 'I was also counting on the support of the leaders of public opinion, but this was not forthcoming. To me it seems elementary that to have accepted the conditions imposed [by the FLQ kidnappers] would have meant a landslide into anarchy ... to have surrendered to such disgusting blackmail, without safeguarding the principle of order which is the basis of the exercise of liberty, would have opened the way to a growth of such methods ... I also expected that there would be no politicking or playing around with such a serious matter as the respect for democratic institutions and the life of a man. I overestimated the powers of comprehension of our leaders of opinion.' (National Assembly of Quebec, 12 Nov. 1970) Despite this, it is worth recalling that even Claude Ryan's *Le Devoir* held suspect the FLQ's lawyer, Robert Lemieux, 'and his friends' for making appeals 'in the streets,' and supported the Bourassa government's calling in of the army: 'To do otherwise would have been to overlook its duty' (*Le Devoir*, 16 Oct. 1970).
42 National Assembly of Quebec, 12 Nov. 1970

night arrests, searches, or the framing of court charges. One wonders, thus, whether the act was proclaimed in 1970 principally for political purposes rather than for the 'special' police powers required for eliminating the threat of escalating disorder. Apart from the retroactive feature respecting FLQ membership (whose purposes could certainly have been achieved under the seditious conspiracy clauses of the Criminal Code) and the provision of detention for up to twenty-one days before a charge was required to be laid, the Criminal Code, together with both police and judicial precedents concerning warrants, searches, and arrests, and even the use of soldiers as police, would probably have sufficed. This seems the more likely when one considers the rapid judicial disposition of the cases against those who were arrested. Within two months 403 of the 465 persons arrested were released without charges being laid.[43] All charges laid under the War Measures Act were stayed by *nolle prosequi* in July 1971 at the request of the Quebec attorney general. Eighty-six people had been charged under the act and sixty-two under sections of the Criminal Code. Only five of those charged under the act, and who pleaded not guilty, were convicted.

Still other aspects of the FLQ crisis suggest comparison with 1919 and also indicate continuities within a Canadian political-legal tradition. While in Winnipeg opinion was evenly and deeply divided with respect to the suppression of 'apprehended insurrection,' the reverse was the case in 1970–1. In fact, not only FLQ members were surprised by the public rallying behind the governmental response to the crisis. Dedicated civil libertarians were also shaken by the overwhelming majorities that endorsed the dramatic, unmistakable reassertion of the principle that order must underlie liberty – in Montreal's civic elections, in Quebec federal by-elections, in legislative votes in Quebec City and Ottawa, and in post-crisis opinion polls. Most Canadians, inside Quebec as well as outside, seemed to agree that the portentous political symbol of the War Measures Act had been required. Partly because this quickly became evident, partly because administration of the Public Order Proclamation was submitted to parliamentary review,[44] and partly because Quebec courts firmly rejected attempts to

43 Those who could prove damage resulting from an arrest that did not culminate in charges were offered compensation. For a summary of the cases see House of Commons *Debates* (7 June 1972), at 2926. A more detailed survey of the court cases and their results appeared in the *Globe and Mail* (CP) (26 July 1973), at 8. Federal and provincial sources differ slightly on numbers of cases in the different categories and even on some dates.

44 Unlike s. 98, the War Measures Act and dependent executive regulations were quickly withdrawn once the crisis was past.

destroy their credibility (the obscenities of the Montreal Five and of Robert Lemieux failed to reproduce the environment of Judge Hoffman's Chicago court), the political aftermath of the crisis and trials was markedly different from that of Winnipeg. Whereas the west compensated radical labour electorally, the radical *nationalistes* in Quebec received a sharp post-crisis rebuff. On the other hand, there was one important, if subtle, similarity. In both cases there was a renewed emphasis on political as opposed to direct action. In Quebec the combined effect on public opinion of terrorism, unacceptable behaviour in court, and the powerful reassertion by the state of the principles of order and legitimacy produced at least verbal recommitment to the electoral process by most sectors of the *nationaliste* 'left' – although in the case of Pierre Vallières 'conversion' may be more accurate than 'recommitment.'

CASES OF LENIENCY

If Canadian courts have been quick to endorse and expound the reasons for vigorous state action in rejecting actual or threatened violence as a political method, a corollary seems to be that they will condone such action only if all non-violent media of criticism and redress of grievance remain unimpeded. This is best illustrated by our two most significant cases involving political freedom of the press. The first of these cases arose when Joseph Howe published in his newspaper, *The Novascotian* (1 January 1835), a letter signed 'The People' which accused the Halifax magistracy and police of having 'taken from the pockets of the people, in over exactions, fines etc., a sum that would exceed, in the gross amount, £30,000.' Since Nova Scotia at that time had no municipal corporations the 'Magistracy' was in fact the city government of Halifax, and Howe had published a blanket accusation against all who had held office in that government over a thirty-year period. He was immediately charged with criminal libel (for clearly political purposes) and came before a court presided over by Chief Justice Haliburton.[45] Howe chose to conduct his own defence because each of the lawyers he consulted advised him that the offending letter was definitely libellous and he should plead guilty. 'The lawyers' observed Howe 'were all very civil, but laughed at me a great deal, quoting the old maxim that "he who pleads his own case has a fool for a client." But the laugh was against them when it was all over.'[46]

45 For an account of the Howe libel case see Chisholm *Speeches and Public Letters of Joseph Howe* (1909).
46 Ibid, at 24

With the aid of books borrowed from the sceptical lawyers, Howe prepared a speech that took him six hours to deliver in court. Although the common law seemed to require that a publisher's intention should be judged solely by the words printed, Haliburton permitted Howe great latitude in developing his argument that the public weal, rather than malice, had been his intention in publishing the letter. In his address Howe touched upon a great many British precedents and remarked that 'I have felt that this case ought to turn on no mere technicality or nice doctrine of law, but on those broad and simple principles of truth and justice to which an unpractised speaker may readily appeal, and which an impartial jury can as clearly comprehend.' Far from being unpractised, Howe was an accomplished and popular speaker, a leading reformer who had very much the common touch, for all his rhetorical flourishes.[47] Commenting on his courtroom experience he wrote to a friend, 'I became conscious that I was commanding the attention of the court and the jury. I was much cheered when I saw the tears rolling down one old gentleman's cheek. I thought he would not convict me if he could help it. I scarcely expected a unanimous verdict, as two or three of the jurors were connections, more or less remote, of some of the justices.'

One of the main reasons for the unanimous verdict to acquit was the legal neutrality of the chief justice, who advised the jury on the law and the facts as he saw them without expressing strong views on the merits of the action. More important was Howe's success in politicizing a case that the claimants had hoped to win on the simple ground of criminality. Following the acquittal all the Halifax magistrates resigned, and in 1841, when Howe was in the provincial cabinet, Halifax was incorporated, receiving 'municipal privileges.' While one might argue that this was an instance in which a court was used as the instrument for securing basic political-social change, Howe's own interpretation is probably more accurate, that is, that the court was used to defend an established political principle and the proper methods of securing substantive change were those of the party system and responsible government.

47 Howe received much hospitality during his frequent politicking journeys around the province. He was known to come into a friend's house of a cold winter evening, turn his back to the fire, and, with considerable informality, break wind. No doubt the jurors were also impressed by Howe's more formal aspects, as when he concluded his address thus: 'Will you permit the sacred fire of liberty, brought by your fathers from the venerable temples of Britain, to be quenched and trodden out on the simple altars they have raised?' In both style and impact Howe's address could be compared to W.J. Bryan's Cross of Gold speech.

While Fred Dixon was charged with seditious, rather than criminal, libel, the nature and significance of his trial in 1920 make it in many respects similar to the Howe case. The sequence of events in 1919 was simple and logical. On 17 June, William Ivens, editor of the *Western Labour News*, was arrested, along with the other Strike Committee leaders, and charged with seditious conspiracy. J.S. Woodsworth and Fred Dixon immediately took over the strikers' newspaper, with Woodsworth as nominal editor. When the paper published, on 23 June, reports of the police-military action of 21 June and editorials denouncing governmental policy as 'Kaiserism' A.J. Andrews immediately arrested Woodsworth, charging him with seditious libel and forbidding further publication of the newspaper.[48] Dixon took over the editorship, and three days later he also was arrested and charged with the same crime. Dixon consulted E.J. McMurray, lawyer for the eight arrested strike leaders, and was advised that it would be best for him to conduct his own defence in court. McMurray was influenced, in offering this excellent advice, by his knowledge of the Howe case. In addition to referring Dixon to John Milton and numerous English precedents he urged him to study the biography of Howe.[49] McMurray evidently recognized in Dixon the 'tribune' type.

An exponent of the single tax, industrial unionism, social democracy, and anti-militarism, Dixon had, like Howe, the common touch. Unlike Howe he had achieved political literacy from the bottom up. Born in England, Dixon was a landscape gardener by trade and an avid, self-educated reader. Supporting nearly every aspect of the progressivism of the period, he was elected to the Manitoba legislature with a large majority in 1914 and an increased majority in 1915, while in 1920 more than 80 per cent of the voters in the proportional representation constituency of Winnipeg put his name on the ballot. His trial occurred in January 1920 in an assize court presided over by the very hostile Judge Galt and a jury composed chiefly of potentially sceptical farmers. During the trial, which lasted sixteen days and resulted in acquittal, Dixon developed an outstanding defence of press freedom.[50]

In both the Howe and Dixon cases, appeals to English common law

---

48 The following letter was sent to the Winnipeg Printing and Engraving Company: 'Gentlemen: Certain numbers of the Western Labour News Special Strike Edition have contained objectionable matter in that it is seditious, inflammatory and inciting to riot, and publication must be discontinued. Yours truly, (sgd.) Alfred J. Andrews, Agent, Department of Justice.'

49 Information gained from an interview with the Hon. E.J. McMurray KC, June 1948

50 See *Dixon's Address to the Jury* Labour Defence Committee (1920).

precedents were decisive, and this perhaps suggests comparison with such cases as those of the other Winnipeg strike leaders and with *R.* v *Buck*, which turned specifically on interpretations of the Canadian Criminal Code. The two press cases reveal one important continuity in the Canadian political tradition – a self-confidence which permits quick action by the state, tempered by comparative lenience and a conviction that legitimacy is strengthened by keeping open the avenues of constitutional criticism.

This line of argument could be further substantiated by reference to a large number of cases involving the relations of Canadian citizens to foreign powers and of aliens to the Canadian state. In such cases, and they include extradition, espionage, invasion, co-operation with invaders, and use of Canada as a base of operations against another state, the courts have often had to attempt definition of 'an offence of a political character.' The recent extradition case of Karl Armstrong, *Re State of Wisconsin and Armstrong*,[51] tends to confirm the leading 1890 case, *Ex parte Castioni*,[52] by revealing a long-standing tendency of Canadian courts to view the use of violence, particularly if death results, as illegitimate political activity and, by implication, more criminal than political. On the other hand, even in cases involving high treason or espionage, once the crisis is past, exceptional care with respect to evidence and comparative leniency both in convicting and sentencing seem the rule. Even the Ancaster 'Bloody Assize' of 1814 received its popular appellation largely from John Beverley Robinson's political opponents.[53] Given extensive Upper Canadian collaboration with the enemy in 1813, especially by the American-born, the policy of Robinson, who was then twenty-two years old and acting attorney general, appears almost startlingly benign. The nineteen accused men had been captured while aiding American raiders in November and December

---

51 (1973) 10 C.C.C. (2d) 271 (Fed. C.A.); leave to appeal to Supreme Court of Canada dismissed 5 March 1973

52 60 L.J. 22. In this case, Denman J remarked, 'I think that in order ... to avoid extradition for such an act as ... murder ... it must be at least shewn that the act which is done is being done in furtherance of, and as a sort of overt act in the course of and with the intention of assisting in a political matter, such as a political rising consequent upon a great dispute between two parties in the State as to which is to have the government in its hands.' I am indebted for this reference to Professor Charles Dalfen.

53 The best account of the Special Court of Oyer and Terminer held in June 1814 is Riddell, 'The Ancaster "Bloody Assize" of 1814,' in Zaslow *The Defended Border: Upper Canada and the War of 1812* (1964). Riddell remarks: 'Robinson was often charged in times a little later with pressing the charges too strongly ... but there is no evidence that he acted more vindictively than was supposed at the time to be the duty of a Crown Counsel. His political enemies did not scruple to call this Assize the "Bloody Assize" and to compare it, very unjustly, to the Bloody Assize of the infamous Jeffreys.'

1813. Two of them were American citizens of whom Robinson remarked that even though they were residents of Upper Canada and thus in law guilty of high treason it would be 'better not to strain the law to its utmost rigor.'[54] In the end the mandatory sentence of hanging was carried out on only eight of the nineteen prisoners.[55] Similarly in 1838-9, when Upper Canadian jails were overflowing with captured American invaders who had thought to complete the liberation work botched by Mackenzie and Papineau, Governor Arthur unconditionally pardoned ninety of the two hundred and twenty prisoners.[56] Seventeen were executed, although Arthur expressed deep repugnance to any capital punishments and allowed them only because it seemed to him 'to be absolutely necessary as awful examples to deter ... a repetition of aggressions.'

In the cases arising from the Kellock-Taschereau royal commission which investigated the espionage revealed by Igor Gouzenko in 1946 a similar pattern may be discerned. As a result of the commission's in camera hearings and its published report, some nineteen people were charged with violation of, and conspiracy to violate, the Official Secrets Act – by providing various kinds of military information to agents operating out of the Russian embassy in Ottawa. For reasons which ranged from inadmissibility of some in camera evidence and alteration of indictment to inconclusive evidence, eight of the nineteen were acquitted (one on appeal), while the heaviest sentence (ten years) was meted out to Alan Nunn May by an English court. To any layman having read the Kellock-Taschereau report this seems a high point of judicial caution and of ultimate leniency.[57]

CONCLUSION

While this discussion of the historical significance of Canadian political trials has been wide-ranging it has also been extremely selective. There is

---

54 Ibid, at 246
55 Thirty other persons received judgments of outlawry, *in absentia*, and some of their lands were forfeited to the crown.
56 See Corey *The Crisis of 1830–1842 in Canadian-American Relations* (1941), at 113ff. Explaining his policy, Arthur remarked during a public speech, 'I frankly avow to you that it has been with me an object of great anxiety to call forth a generous feeling from those who have acted toward this country with cruel treachery and wanton violence. If the endeavor be successful ... it will be to me a source of unbounded satisfaction.'
57 Results of the 'Gouzenko cases' were summarized by the Department of Justice for insertion in copies of the Kellock-Taschereau Report in 1958. See also *Rex v Gerson*, [1948] 3 D.L.R. 280 (Ont. C.A.), for a discussion of 'amendment of indictment.' For parliamentary discussion of these cases, see House of Commons *Debates* (1947), vol. 4, at 3156, and Mackenzie King's statement, 18 March 1946.

certainly room for a vast amount of quantitative research to include, for example, hundreds of cases in which the courts have rendered verdicts and expounded political-social philosophy in actions which were not originally or specifically political, as well as many which were political even by a narrow definition. Many cases involving such matters as industrial conflict, extradition and other foreign relations, anti-trust action, courts martial, or religious rights exhibit political attitudes both current and inherited. The present selective survey may serve to suggest guidelines for the formulation of hypotheses.

On the basis of this discussion it may be argued that our courts, in dealing with clearly political cases, have both reflected and expounded a confidence in the legitimacy of an evolving Canadian society and especially in the political-legal principles of that society. Thus they have firmly rejected the use of violence by any entity other than the state. So, too, they have resisted any effort to make them the agents of social change or to destroy the trial process by disruptive politicization. One result of these consistent attitudes has been positive encouragement of democratic party organization and, indeed, of a multi-party system which is distinctively Canadian.[58] Judicial insistence on the legitimacy of established authority, nourished by retention of the symbols and precedents of constitutional monarchy, has often, of course, worked to the advantage of social-economic elites.[59] But where this has been the case, changes in the structure of power and the distribution of wealth have been sought, often effectively, through democratic political action. Moreover, if the courts have been quick to lend support to established authority in real or alleged crisis situations and thus have appeared to be an arm of the executive, their severity has often been mitigated by executive-legislative policy – deciding, for example, who should actually be prosecuted, reprieved, or compensated.

Finally, although the courts have resisted any temptation to propound advanced ideas in social-economic policy, it would be absurd to argue that they have simply reflected a Canada that is a Lockean fragment frozen in

58 The federal multiethnic nature of the country is, of course, a primary factor, but upon this the attitude of the courts toward the legitimacy of political methods has acted as a catalyst.

59 Propriety in court procedure, on the other hand, together with a careful regard for press freedom (but not including freedom of 'contempt'), have often benefited accused persons – as in the Gouzenko cases or even the FLQ cases. In Jacques Rose's third trial, for example, the judge was quick to investigate claims made by the jury that 'plainclothes agents' tried to infiltrate the jury and were spying upon and 'hassling' the jurors. See *Globe and Mail* (17 July 1973), at 1.

unchanging political attitudes. What the courts *have* reflected is an unchanging Canadian belief in constitutionality against a background of political adaptation to the changing requirements of an increasingly industrial society. There is a wide gap in political philosophy between, say, Chief Justice Robinson expounding the duties and benefits of the 'middle station of life' and Chief Justice Laskin on the duties of multinational corporations with respect to their unionized employees. Yet Robinson, like most of his more liberal successors, would also have approved the use of the War Measures Act in 1970.

KENNETH MCNAUGHT, a graduate of the University of Toronto, is a professor of history at the University of Toronto. He is a well-known commentator on public affairs and the author of numerous articles in scholarly and popular journals. He has written six books, the most recent being *The Winnipeg General Strike* (1974) and the *Pelican History of Canada* (1969).

Canadian University Paperbooks
of related interest

Lightning Source UK Ltd.
Milton Keynes UK
UKHW010000210722
406167UK00001B/252

9 780802 062734